To Michele

Summer School 2011

CW01617565

Toledo Blade

By

Anthony Clive

Anthony Clive

By the same author

In the Voravia Series:

Toledo Blade

A Pale Horse

His Nation's Champion

Firepower

Winter

Printed editions available from Amazon

e-books from Kindle, i-Books, Kobo & Nook

Coming soon:
Rebellion

Published by Anthony Clive under licence to
Brown Dog Books, 7 Green Park Station, Bath BA1 1JB

www.selfpublishingpartnership.co.uk

ISBN 978-1-903056-57-8

Printed and bound by CPI Group (UK) Ltd,
Croydon CR0 4YY

For Tilly

Contents

Part Two

Crown and Sceptre: Princess Lucia of Voravia

Map of Southern Voravia

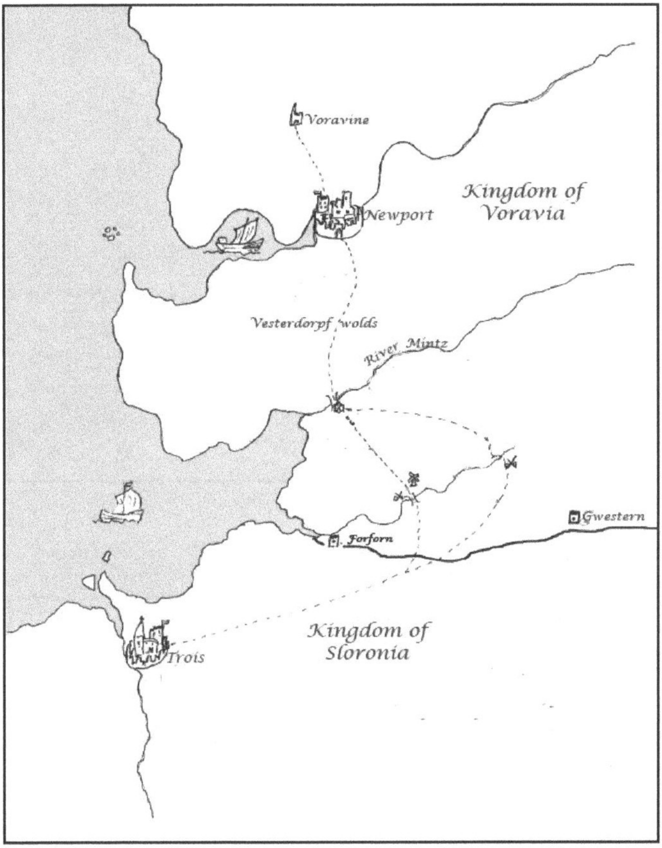

Map of Nieuport

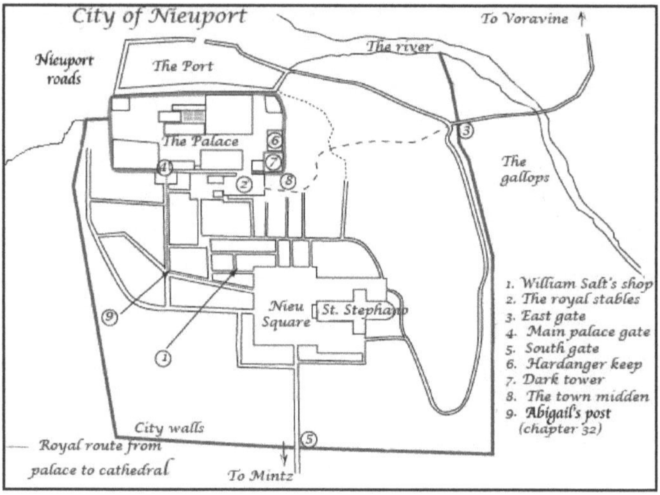

Plan of royal palace

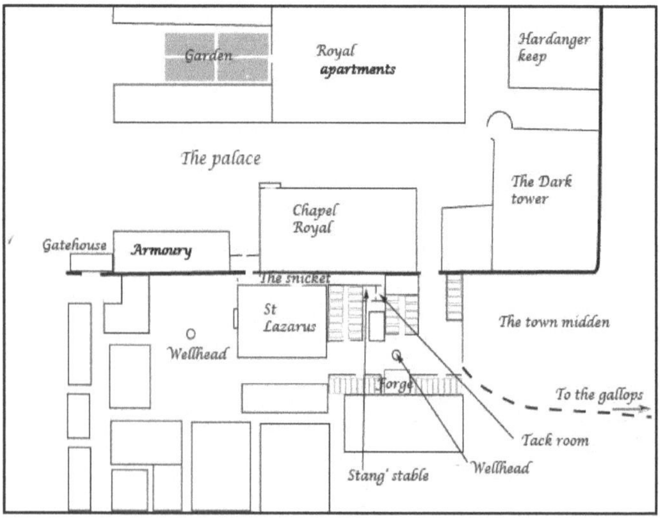

Royal families

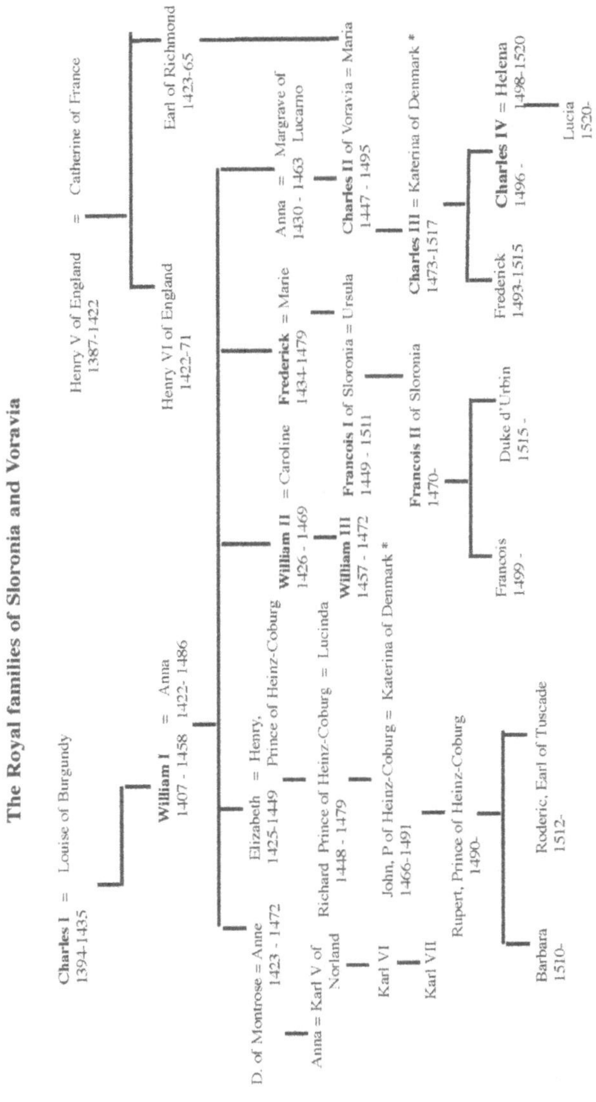

Historical note - A Toledo blade

The Spanish city of Toledo lies 45 miles south of Madrid.

In classical times the Toledo iron swords, now known as *falcata*, were used by Hannibal and later adopted by the Roman centurions. Subsequently, by incorporating a small amount of carbon, the iron was turned into the stronger metal we know as steel. Heating, hammering and plunging the steel into water hardens it and it was the exceptional hardness of the steel that distinguished Toledo blades from others.

The city continued to dominate the production of swords for a thousand years. It is known that El Cid the liberator of Spain from Moorish rule and Pizarro, the sixty year old, illiterate conquistador of Peru carried Toledo blades.

Toledo swords were the weapons of choice for all who could afford them. The Count di Montelucca, as a full time professional soldier of fortune, would almost certainly carry one, possibly from the famous forge of Juan and Gil Alman.

We are not told the name of the swordsmith who made Peter Salt's Toledo blade.

Part One

*

Horse and Sword

Peter Salt

'Before all else, be armed.'
Niccolò Machiavelli

Chapter 1

THE VISIT

Peter Salt looked up and down the street. The cobbles glittered from the recent shower. At the far end a solitary figure appeared to be searching for an address. Closer at hand two scrawny gutter-curs snarled and snapped over a heap of pig's intestines. Further down, where Whitefriars Street joined the great square, a small group was gathered, possibly listening to a friar preaching the Gospel but just as likely, to an itinerant pedlar extolling the virtues of his cure-all, a sure remedy for everything from boils to inflammation of the spleen. These apart, the street was deserted.

He slid the bolts across the door to the apothecary's shop.

When he returned, his father had already begun to grind a sample of ore with his pestle and mortar. The acrid reek of sulphur stung his throat.

'Last Wednesday an Italian trader sold me this lump of brimstone. I doubt it has any medical properties but I have a curiosity about it. The Church teaches us that it will, together with fire, be part of the torment of sinful souls in hell. So let us see how much substance there is in the threat. Go and get a slice from that fine ham your mother is drying.'

Peter was about to go to the larder when there came a loud rap on the door. He glanced nervously at his father. If this were one of Archbishop Godwin's spies they were in trouble. To be caught in an experiment that questioned the traditional teaching of the Church could be seen as witchcraft. Witches were burnt.

The knock was repeated and then a voice called out.

'William Salt, please open to a friend.'

Peter hesitated to allow William time to gather up the scientific equipment and place it on a shelf behind a curtain. He opened the door.

The man who entered was the one Peter had seen earlier. He was soberly dressed and so tall he had to stoop to pass under the lintel. He walked through the shop, into the parlour and took off his large hat to reveal a face with strong features. An auburn beard, flecked with grey, could not hide the pits and scars that told of a childhood attack of smallpox, the illness that, five years ago, had carried off Peter's two little sisters in one dreadful week.

It took William a second or two to recognise their visitor. Then he made a hurried bow and said, 'Peter, 'tis King Charles. Pay your respects.'

'Oh, I'm supposed to be in disguise,' the king laughed. 'Perhaps, Master Salt, you would introduce me to your family.'

William led the way through into the kitchen that also served as parlour and beckoned his wife, Abigail, to come forward. She made a rather clumsy kind of curtsy as the king offered her his hand. As soon as she could, she scuttled back to her corner. Then William introduced his son to the king. Peter shook his sovereign's hand solemnly.

'Mrs Salt, I wonder if you have two drinking vessels

in this delightfully snug room so your husband and I could enjoy a glass of wine together. I've brought a flask of claret that I think he'll enjoy.'

Abigail opened an oak cupboard and found two pewter tankards.

'William,' the king began, 'every day for the past decade I have remembered my debt to you. I have never properly repaid it. I mean to do that one day, but now I have come to ask a further favour.' He paused, poured a measure of wine into the two tankards. 'Your good health.'

Peter watched as his father sampled the wine. He guessed it was the best he had ever had.

The king turned to Abigail. 'I don't suppose William has ever told you of the great service he did me ten years ago.' He paused but Abigail was too nervous to reply. 'It was then that my dear wife, Queen Helena, went into labour with our first child. All sorts of complications set in and the midwives and my doctor didn't know what to do. He sent for four of his colleagues. They tried everything in their powers, mostly, if you ask my opinion, superstitious nonsense and procedures hallowed more by tradition than good science.' The king shook his head. 'Eventually I had to accept that my wife would not survive and that the chances for our child were slight. I decided to send for the one man I knew who would bring a scientific approach. I sent for your William. How I wished I'd done so earlier. When he arrived he requested the so-called men of medicine to withdraw and proceeded to deliver the babe. He gave the girl to my dear wife to hold for a few minutes and then she drifted away. I can still see the soft smile on her lips as she held our tiny daughter. I like to think she died happy.'

There followed an awkward silence, then the king continued in a brighter tone, 'Now William, let me top up your wine. Then I'll explain my idea.'

When both tankards had been refilled, the king asked for a seat and said, 'My Lucy is now eleven years old. She's a fine healthy child and I'm sure one day she'll be as beautiful as her mother was. I shan't have a son; so when I've gone she will sit on my throne. It will not be easy for her, nor will her life be without danger. I should know. Ever since we broke away from Sloronia - when was it? It must be over a hundred years ago - my family has had to contend with threats and plots. My brother Frederick's death was never fully explained and there have been at least three attempts on my life. It would be no surprise if Sloronia were not looking for another opportunity as we speak.'

'Your Majesty, I had no idea you were in danger here in Nieuport,' William said.

The king shrugged. 'I should be more worried than I am, I suppose, but I've grown quite sanguine. I've been lucky to date, in that respect anyway. Now to my Lucy. I've seen to it that my girl has received the best education and training that money can buy. She's a good reader, knows quite a lot of Latin and has a good knowledge of the scriptures. She dances, plays the lute and she rides well. So, you see, I've prepared her for the life of a lady at court. But she will be more, much more, than a lady at court. She will have to govern Voravia.'

William nodded.

'To do that she will need to be at the forefront of this new scientific learning that is sweeping our world. I've been racking my brains to think how this can be achieved and, I believe, I've come up with the answer. I want to arrange for Lucia to spend two hours every day in your house where she is to be taught.'

The king took another pull at his wine and continued, 'I expect you're wondering why I want her instruction to take place here rather than at the palace. Well, at the palace, nobles and courtiers surround her, whereas here she will be with real people. People who are more honest and less affected than those at Court. So, in studying here, I believe she will learn to respect the good people of our realm as well as the latest thinking. In return for your teaching Lucy and perhaps as a way of partly repaying my debt, I suggest your Peter attends lessons with her both here and at the palace. It will be easier for her if she has a school-friend to study with and it'll be pleasant for me to have a young lad about the palace. Come to think of it, I might even give him a few lessons in the knightly skills. Well, what do you say to my idea?'

Would his father accept? He could hardly refuse his king. Peter waited as William sat for a few seconds whilst he took in the offer.

'Your Majesty, I can't begin to tell you the honour you pay me. I'm sure you could find greater scholars than me. As soon as the princess is old enough you should consider enrolling her at one of the great universities. But, until that day, I think I could give her an enthusiasm for science. I accept your offer. When had you in mind for the lessons to begin?'

King Charles leapt to his feet, seized William's hand and shook it heartily.

Then he raised his tankard and called out, 'A toast to science!'

William raised his tankard and the two men drank.

'People accuse me of impetuosity,' the king said, 'but I believe in striking whilst the iron is hot. Let's start tomorrow. Now, young man, how old are you?'

'I am soon to be twelve, sir.'

'And how are your reading skills and your mathematics?'

'They are quite fair, my lord. I can read most words. I understand Latin and I have a smattering of Greek.'

'Well in the latter case you have the advantage over me. I have never mastered that most classical of languages. I come from what I believe scholars, such as your father, refer to as the dark ages.'

The king refilled his tankard and sat back in his chair. There was a silence, then he laughed. 'You've no idea, Mrs Salt, how pleasant all this is. Here I am in this jolly household, in good company. And there's a delicious smell of cooking. Is that a rabbit you have there in the pot? I thought so. I just don't know how many years it is since I last had a good rabbit stew. I seem to live on nothing but complicated over-rich stuff, except when I am campaigning. Then it's more often than not silverbrord and stale bread.' The king paused and then added, 'I've nothing against a tasty piece of our national sausage, but I can assure you it can become most monotonous.'

'I'm sure Abigail can add some more vegetables and perhaps find a piece of ham, my lord, if you would care to join us for supper.' William had taken the only too obvious hint.

'If that's an invitation, I accept it. But let me at least contribute. Peter, go up to the palace. Give them this note and bring back another bottle of this claret your father seems to be appreciating.'

The king opened his scrip and took out a piece of paper. He wrote a few words on it, signed it with a flourish and dated it 3 October 1530. Then he unbuttoned the top of his jerkin and took from around his neck a seal, which he pressed onto the paper. 'There, that will be sufficient authority. Now run up to the lower gate. Ask for my steward and wait for the wine.'

Peter examined the impression the seal had made in the paper. It showed, in relief, the arms of Voravia - two griffins supporting a shield with four crowned swans and a salmon. Below the arms were the initials C IV. He folded the slip of paper, tucked it into his belt and set off up the narrow twisting Street of the Whitefriars towards the great castle. He had not gone far when he heard the familiar but sad clang of a small bell and a rattle.

He withdrew into an alley to let the little file of

lepers pass. They came quite close and he cowered back, fearful that he would be contaminated. One of the lepers held out a begging cup. Peter felt into the pocket of his breeches and found only the one coin - a half groat. He hesitated for a moment, for it was rather a large amount, then decided that, with the king in his house, he should be generous. He tossed the coin towards the cup. It hit the side and fell to the ground. The leper stooped to pick it up. His fingers, deadened by the effects of his condition, scrabbled in the dirt for the coin. He managed to collect it and turned a face, eaten away by disease, to mouth his thanks.

Chapter 2

TWO PIGEONS

Peter arrived at the outer gate where a guard stepped out and asked his business. Peter showed him the slip of paper and the guard, who could not conceal his surprise to see the seal of King Charles upon it, allowed him to enter.

He looked about him for someone to ask. A tough-looking man, dressed in leather, stood at a tiny doorway in a grim building set into one of the castle's walls. As there was no one else about, Peter went over to him and asked him if he was the king's steward.

'What me? No, I'm the gaoler.' The man laughed.

'Well, sir, can you tell me where I'd find the steward, please?'

"Ain't often anyone calls me sir. Mostly 'tis "do this Vladimar, fetch that Vladimar". Anyways, that's the door you want.' He jerked his head in the direction.

As Peter walked towards the door, a group of five boys, who he judged to be about two years older than he was, came round a corner. Their clothes, although subdued, were stylish and clearly expensive. They walked with the swagger and confidence of the nobility. Peter stepped to one side to allow them to pass.

'Hello, what have we here?' the leading one asked.

‘God knows, Ferdinand. Looks like some little peasant,’ one of his companions replied, giving Peter a sharp poke with his cane.

‘No, Richard, I think not. More likely some grubby little tradesman’s brat.’

Conditioned by his upbringing to expect condescension and frequently outright abuse from the aristocracy, Peter took another step back.

‘Well, didn’t your parents tell you to bow to your betters?’ The boy called Ferdinand thrust his face forward towards Peter.

Peter gave a peremptory nod of his head, his temper rising and his fists clenching.

‘And take your cap off. Or do you want me to teach you some manners?’ Ferdinand grabbed Peter’s cap and hurled it into the middle of the court.

Blind with anger and forgetting that he was outnumbered and much younger, Peter jabbed a punch at Ferdinand.

Ferdinand easily warded off the blow. ‘You’re going to regret that after I’ve finished with you. I’m going to give you such a flogging you won’t be able to sit down for a week. Bend him over, you two. We’ll teach urchins like him to stick to their own dirty little part of town.’

Before he could escape, Peter was seized, hauled into a corner between two buildings and his breeches dragged down.

‘Lend me your cane, Richard, if you don’t mind its being sullied by its proximity to a commoner’s arse.’

Peter bit his lip. He was not going to cry out as

Ferdinand, grunting with the effort, thrashed his behind and upper thighs. The beating would have lasted longer had not Vladimar arrived.

'Oi, what's goin' on 'ere? You leave that lad alone. 'e ain't 'alf your size.'

As Peter gingerly pulled his breeches up over his weals, the group of pages sauntered off, Ferdinand and Richard arm in arm and laughing.

'Thinks they own the world, them do. You alright?'

Peter nodded. Waves of pain flooded through him.

'Well, then you'd better get on with yer business'

The door Vladimar had pointed to was partly ajar. Peter cautiously entered it.

'Hello, is there anybody there?'

After a few minutes a smartly dressed man appeared and Peter handed him the note. Once again it was received with surprise and the footman left to return with an old, stout and comfortable-looking gentleman who must be the king's steward.

He looked at Peter's note and smiled. 'His Majesty likes these little forays into the city. Sometimes he goes unrecognised but I suspect, more often than not, he is detected. Still, it does give him a chance to meet his subjects and he must learn a little about the world beyond these walls or the battlefield. Now then, young man, let me see what I must get. He asks for two bottles of the finest claret and a pair of pigeons. We'll see what we can find. It'll take a few minutes. The king further suggests you might like to see the library.'

He turned to the footman and told him to show Peter the collection of books.

Peter followed the footman, thinking how much he would have preferred to see the horses but, when the library door was unlocked with a great key, he knew that here was a room his father would love to visit.

The books were displayed on tables or on shelves and looked to be of enormous value. Most were in Latin and many gorgeously illuminated. Peter had never seen anything like them. In one corner of the room there was a desk with a large window behind it. Peter walked over to the window and looked out. Below was a small court, with a parterre of clipped box hedges. The low watery sun poured through the glass onto the desk and a quick glance showed that this was where Princess Lucia had her schooling. There was a jar of fresh roses, their perfume mingling with that of leather. So this would be his classroom. What a wonderful place to study. Already the pain of his beating seemed to be fading.

The footman came over to him quite deferentially and told him that the steward had returned with the wine and the birds. Peter took the bag, thanked the old man and left the way he had entered. His mother, who he knew had been worried not only at entertaining royalty but whether she had enough food to do so, would be delighted with the two birds.

Peter retraced his steps; there was no sign of the lepers. After the enormous size of everything within the castle, the streets and houses of Nieuport seemed tiny and haphazard.

He pushed open the door to the shop and was struck by the contrast with the library. That room had been light and airy. It had been perfumed with rich leather and roses. His house was small and musty. It smelt of damp, brimstone and his father's wares and, every so often, the stench from the communal latrine in the yard. He was ashamed of the meanness of everything and dreaded what King Charles must be thinking.

He need not have worried. The king may have been unaccustomed to so tight a space or the stink of everyday life, but it did not seem to have affected his humour. He was in the best of spirits and even Abigail was beginning to enjoy herself. The sight of the two pigeons, already plucked and drawn, removed her last worry. They were hastily threaded on the spit and a delicious smell of roasting fowl filled the room.

A second bottle of wine was broached - the king insisted on giving the third one to the Salts by way of thanks for his supper - and the conversation between monarch and citizens flowed in as relaxed a way as could be imagined. The two main subjects discussed were the education of women, about which the king had strong views - girls should be given the same opportunities as boys - and the importance of scientific research about which everyone agreed.

Then Abigail laid four wooden plates on the table, placed a knife beside each and put a warm loaf in the centre of the table. She lifted the pot off the fire and put it in front of the king's place.

'No, no,' the king cried out, 'let the head of the house first say grace and then serve.'

The four sat with their heads bowed as William asked God's blessing on Voravia, his house and the food. Then he began to serve. Of course he served his guest first and selected the best pieces. But when the king had received his plate he said, 'This should be Abigail's portion. I say we give the best cuts to she who has done all the work.'

Then he added, 'As for young Peter, as he is still growing, let his portion include the most nutritious parts.'

Peter received the liver, heart and kidneys.

The king busied himself with cutting the bread. Then two mugs were filled with small ale from the pantry and the men's tankards re-filled.

After a couple of mouthfuls, the king wiped his mouth on his sleeve, raised his tankard and declared. "Mistress Salt, this is most delicious. If this is how the Salt family eat, I shall consider vacating my palace for life here in Whitefriars."

The pieces of rabbit were picked up and the meat chewed off the bone. The king picked up the head and cracked it open with the hasp of his knife to suck out the delicious brains. Then the juices were mopped up with bread.

Next came the pigeons, now roasted, followed by four apples. At the end of the feast the king called another toast to Abigail Salt and leaned back in his chair, almost dislodging the scientific equipment.

'I can honestly say I've not enjoyed an afternoon and evening as much as this for ages.'

The church bells broke up the discussion and it was agreed that Peter should present himself at the lower gate at eight the next day.

That evening the Salts attended their local church and returned to a darkened house.

It was as Peter was about to go upstairs to bed that his father took him to one side.

'While you were at the palace the king enlarged on his fears for his daughter. He asked me to speak to you about it. There is, as you know, only the one heir to the throne, the Princess Lucia. If anything happens to her it is not at all clear who would succeed. This means that there is every incentive for any ambitious man with a possible claim, to plot against the princess. Of course the king does everything within his power to protect the girl, not only out of love but also for the sake of the nation, but he can't be with her all the time. And he has to accept that as she grows older she'll expect more independence. He told me he's no wish to curb what is natural in any young person. He would like her to have a friend in whom she can confide. Someone more her own age. Someone who will, to his best ability, keep an eye out for danger. He has taken a liking to you and feels you might be the right person. He told me, and Peter this was awkward for him, that he wanted someone from among the ordinary people, like us, who wouldn't be in a position to er... to woo her. For diplomatic reasons, she will, one day, have to marry some neighbouring prince. Such, the king explained, are the burdens of royalty. Peter, this is an enormous honour and a responsibility. I know you'll do your best.'

Peter did not sleep well. His bruises ached. When he touched them he found they were suppurating blood where the skin had been broken. The prospects for the morrow were worrying. It was not the responsibility of keeping an eye on the princess. That was almost the easiest part although, as the night progressed, he began to ask himself from whom the danger might come. Could it be Vladimar? He seemed rough and tough enough, yet he had shown some kindness. Could it perhaps be one of those unpleasant pages? They were horrible but were probably a bit too young.

The one part of his father's revelation that gave him no anxiety was the ban on wooing the princess. The idea of wooing a princess, or any other girl for that matter, hardly crossed his mind.

Much more frightening was her probable attitude. Judging by his experience with the pages it was likely to be intimidating. Even if she turned out to be as friendly as her father, it was inevitable he would re-meet Ferdinand and his colleagues. They would not miss any chance to humiliate him for his simple manners and lowly birth. He had to accept they were older and stronger than he was. Future meetings were likely to be equally unpleasant.

Chapter 3

BELLE

Peter rose early and dressed in a white linen shirt, his best jerkin of brown serge and hose of dark blue wool. He pushed a bone comb through his tousled hair and put on the black leather shoes with brass buckles his mother had recently purchased.

He ate his bread and slice of silverbrord with a dry mouth and then walked up towards the lower gate clutching his quill pen. There had been more rain in the night but today promised to be one of those warm sunny ones so frequent in late autumn.

How different the streets were on a weekday. Now they were crowded with people and animals. Peter had to dodge packhorses and lumbering oxen hauling drays. There were traders hawking goods and shouting out prices. He stepped aside for two stout housewives each with one hand clutching a basket and the other hitching her skirts to avoid the filth in the street. There were children, still half-asleep, trudging to school. He narrowly avoided being splattered with last night's piss from a pot emptied from above. On one corner the local harlot, even at this early hour dressed in her bright rags, lounged against her doorway whilst she negotiated with a couple of sailors fresh off their ship. Over all hung the smell of smoke from damp wood fires. He arrived as the parish church bell sounded eight.

Peter was met at the gate by a thin young friar in

the black and white garb of the Dominicans. His face was adorned with a wispy beard.

'I am Brother Simon. It is my duty to school the Princess Lucia and His Majesty tells me that you are to join her in her studies. His Majesty also informs me that each afternoon I am to accompany the princess to the house of your father, William Salt, where the princess is to receive instruction in, what His Majesty refers to, as the new learning.'

Peter, much relieved to find he was expected, extended a hand. He received a very limp, damp one in reply.

Brother Simon turned and led the way to the library. He tapped on the door and opened it.

Princess Lucia was seated behind the desk and rose to greet them. She possessed a solemn face with a confident, possibly even arrogant, gaze in her grey-blue eyes. Although she was almost as tall as Peter, she had a very slender build.

Peter, who was half-expecting the princess would be in a magnificent gown with a crown on her head, was surprised to see how she was dressed. She wore a plain white linen gown with a cord around her waist. Her pale hair was brushed back and fell down her back. Her face immediately relaxed and her eyes shone with pleasure at the sight of someone her own age. She stepped round from behind the desk and Peter made a deep bow, something he had been practising since he had risen that morning.

Princess Lucia responded with an accomplished curtsy then laughed.

'Papa tells me that we are to be quite informal. We are to be friends, so let us dispense with bows and curtsies. I find them very unfriendly. And I would prefer it if you address me as Lucy, for that is the name I like.'

Brother Simon indicated a small table that was to be Peter's place of study. Behind it was a plain stool and open upon the table a Bible printed in Voravian. Peter looked at the parchment and the lettering. His father had told him of the new invention but it was the first time he had seen print.

He sat down very delicately, hoping neither Lucy nor Brother Simon would notice the way he clenched his teeth at the sudden pain.

The morning was spent in a study of the letter of St. Paul to the Romans and with translating from Latin a passage from the Roman historian, Livy. Princess Lucia was quite adept at the work and also at teasing poor Brother Simon who was in no little awe of his quick-witted and mischievous young charge.

A midday meal was served in the library consisting of cheese, silverbrord eaten by rich and poor alike but not by Princess Lucia who pushed it aside, and smoked fish with bread and small beer. Then the two young scholars were allowed to take some exercise in the little garden. Lucy danced along the paths and Peter, mindful of both his humble breeding and his two years seniority, walked purposefully around the box hedges. Brother Simon sat himself on a stone seat and took out a small missal and began to read. They had been exercising for only a few minutes when a door opened and out strode King Charles. Lucy ran to him; he kissed her gently and took her hand.

'I am sure Master Salt would like to see the stables,' he said. 'This way, young man.'

They left the garden by a small door, passed through a huge empty hall and out into the main court. They were heading for a gate in the outer wall. As they did so a small group of pages carrying wooden swords came towards them. Peter recognised Ferdinand and his friend amongst them. Seeing the king they halted, stepped aside and bowed, doffing their caps. A look of astonishment crossed Ferdinand's face as he saw Peter was with the king. Peter could not resist giving Ferdinand a long, hard stare followed by an insolent grin.

They passed through the gate and into the yard below the castle walls. Stables surrounded the yard on all sides. Some were finely built of brick or stone, others, presumably for working horses, were more like farm sheds and constructed of wood. In the centre was a wellhead.

The place was busy. Stable lads were leading horses across the cobbles, others were mucking out and one was grooming a beautiful chestnut mare. Turning to their left they walked to a line of doors set into a low building that backed onto the walls of the castle. As they approached a groom met them. 'This is Master Peter Salt, a companion and fellow scholar to the princess; he would like to see the horses. Please be so good as to show them to him.' Once again, Peter was amazed at King Charles' politeness to all he had business with.

The groom led the way into the gloom of the stables. Peter looked in excitement at the splendid animals, each housed in a separate stall. These were unlike the numerous horses he saw about Nieuport bearing traders and farmers. Some, like the swift-looking hunters, must carry the blood of the Arab stallions brought into Voravia over the recent years. Others were great warhorses.

They left the stabling and re-entered the yard. The king led the way down a short passage to a small brick-built building. The groom ran ahead and opened the door and the party entered a dark stable. On the right was a door that was a little ajar and Peter could see it was a tack-room. In front of them was a single stall and within it a huge black horse. High up in the far wall a tiny window, much shrouded in ivy and cobwebs, allowed a shaft of light to illuminate a gloomy roof space of old beams.

'This is my best friend, Stang,' said King Charles. He rubbed Stang's forelock and laughed. 'You and I have been through much, have we not, my old comrade? Whenever I've asked you for one more effort you have never refused me.'

Peter and Lucy looked at the great horse and Lucy whispered to Peter. 'I do believe, if he could, old Stang would tell Papa he did it all for love.'

King Charles turned to Brother Simon. 'I think we can give education a miss for an hour.'

He spoke to the groom. 'Find this young scholar a horse to suit him and let's see what he is made of. His father tells me he loves nothing more than riding.'

The groom walked back and they re-entered the main stable block. He stopped at a stall housing a bay with a narrow nervous-looking head with wild excitable eyes.

'I reckon that there Belle would be just right for the young gen'leman. She be a bit frisky and skittish but she be a lovely ride an', I reckon, she be about his size if he but grow a bit more.'

'She's new, isn't she, Jack?' the king asked.

'Aye, sire. Only had her here these last two months. She be one of Sir Hugh Astley's fillies. Bred out on the downs at his stable two years ago. Got a wonderful pedigree, she has. If she be anything like her dam she'll be wondrous fast.'

'Then Belle it be,' cried the king.

Peter looked at the young mare and felt his heart take a leap. The groom led Belle out of her stall and threw a saddle over her; she flinched and gave a small kick, then allowed the bridle and bit to be fitted. Skittish she certainly was, but brimful of energy.

The groom fixed the stirrups and asked. 'Shall Princess Lucia ride as well?'

'Oh yes, I shall.' The princess was not going to forgo the chance to show her new friend how well she rode.

'Saddle up Tench,' ordered the king. 'Now you two, don't think every day will be devoted to pleasure. You've work to do.'

Unlike the frisky Belle, Tench stood placidly whilst his bridle and saddle were fitted. He appeared to be a quiet, well-behaved pony and very suitable for a young princess. Once he was ready, two grooms led the horses through a gate at the far end of the yard.

They emerged at the head of a steep-sided valley, a part of the town Peter had never visited. A rough track, much pitted with hoof prints, ran down the right side. On their left the ground fell away then rose in an almost sheer grass bank to the foot of the castle wall, forming a natural moat. To their right, a series of little terraces had been constructed to form narrow gardens with the remains of the year's vegetable crops still in evidence. A number of paths ran down between the terraces and these were filled with foul smelling rivulets of household and human waste. Lucy gathered her dress up and hopped across each, wrinkling her nose. The floor of the valley was an odious swamp filled with nettles and coarse grasses. In contrast to the neatness and order of the stabling this seemed to be the city's neglected cesspit. They wound their way down, crossing the main road from the town to the port, and shortly came to a gate in the town walls. Once through it they were on a flat sandy strip that flanked the river that flowed into the estuary.

The groom easily lifted Lucy into her side-saddle where she sat bolt upright with her reins neatly held in her lap. Peter mounted very nervously, caused as much by the fear of this test of his riding skills as the pain of his beating.

He grasped the reins and gave a small kick with his heels. It was as if Belle's hind legs were coiled springs abruptly released. The next moment he was flat on his back on the sand. Lucy's laugh hurt almost more than the fresh impact to his bruises. He scrambled to his feet. Belle stood placidly tugging at a clump of grass. Peter shook his head gritted his teeth and re-mounted. Then they were off. He had hoped to display a competent degree of horsemanship. Instead he was in danger of being ignominiously ditched again. Within seconds he was back to the first time he had been put in the saddle, bent forward and clinging hold of Belle's mane, the tug of which seemed only to impel the mare into greater speed.

Gradually he adjusted to his mount's rhythm. He was able to release his grip on her mane and his heart began to slow. He knew he was going to survive. At last in control, he started to enjoy Belle's speed and responsiveness to the slightest touch. He knew he would never forget the power of that wild dash along the riverbank. He reined Belle in and began to get his breath back. Turning he watched Lucy cantering towards him, her fair hair fluttering out behind her. Way, way back stood the king with his hands on his hips and a smile on his lips.

The two children turned their horses and cantered back side by side. When they were about half way to the king, Lucy gave Tench a light touch of her whip and veered off to the left towards a fallen tree, Peter dug his heels in and followed towards the obstacle. At the last moment Lucy gave a small tug on Tench's bit and he swerved to miss the jump, but Belle took the log in an almost effortless leap. When they pulled up beside the king, the monarch looked up at Peter.

'Well, my boy, how was that? What do you think to our Belle?'

Peter swallowed as he thought frantically of the right way to reply to his King, 'Sir, she is the bravest horse I have ever ridden.'

'As brave as Belle! Yes that has a fine sound. Let it be our motto,' laughed Lucy.

'I don't think I am good enough for her just yet. But sir, I will try to do better,' Peter added.

'Well said. I can see you're a fine horseman. And you're polite as well, a good combination. Now I believe it's high time you two went down to start your instruction in the sciences. Brother Simon's no great enthusiast for the new learning. I suspect he believes it will undermine the teachings of his Church. But it's a poor institution that can't live with man's quest for knowledge. When I say man's, my dear child, I did not mean to exclude woman's.'

The grooms led the two horses away and Brother Simon, now even less at ease after watching the abilities of his two young charges, set off with them through the town towards the apothecary's shop.

Accustomed to the luxury of life at the palace, Lucy was most unlikely to be impressed by what she would find.

Chapter 4

THE PROPERTIES OF WATER

Peter need not have worried about the princess's reaction to the Salts' modest home. Lucy had spent the short walk praising Peter's horsemanship and, when Peter opened the door to the shop, she appeared to be genuinely interested in the various jars and bottles on sale. He introduced Lucy and Brother Simon to William and Abigail, who was as nervous of the girl as she had been of her father.

Then the apothecary explained the method he would follow in his teaching.

'If there is one characteristic that defines the new learning, it is that nothing is true until it is proven. We may say that what distinguishes metals is that they are solid because that is what we observe, but then we come across quicksilver. Is this a metal or a liquid such as water? I hope to teach you that you must take nothing for granted. You must question. You must test. Each year brings new discoveries and many of them contradict the beliefs of the past. Everyone who follows the new learning is making his own contribution. We're as much a part of the progress in thought in this humble apothecary's shop, as the learned doctors at the great universities.'

Peter watched Brother Simon. He stood awkwardly by the door. He seemed not to be sure whether his allegiance lay to Archbishop Godwin or King Charles.

‘We will start by investigating the properties of that very common substance, water. I think we will be quite surprised at how much there is to learn about it.’

William taught largely by suggestion that prompted an answer. To start with, Peter, who was re-treading familiar territory, was the one who responded, but once Brother Simon had made a contribution it was as if the two newcomers had lost their inhibitions. Towards the end of their researches, William placed a pan on Abigail’s stove and quite soon the water was boiling and turning to steam.

It was after a short discussion on the curious way in which a liquid could change its state, that Lucy remarked slowly, ‘So water is not just a liquid like everyone thinks. It can be an air. But what about snow or ice?’

William leaned back and smiled. ‘Princess, you are quite right. That is just how I want you to think. We have shown it can become a vapour, or air as you called it, but we know ice is a solid, and a tremendously strong one. It will bear the weight of a mounted man. Even snow, a substance part way between a liquid and a solid, can form a bridge over a ditch, and, what’s more, the weight of additional snow does not lead to the bridge’s collapse. With a few sticks as a foundation and enough snow the ditch becomes indiscernible. Yet ice and snow, water and steam are only different forms of the same water. Perhaps we can generalise and say that vapour, liquid and solid are but states of the same element.’

By the time the church bells told them that it was six o'clock the four of them had endeavoured to record as many features of water as they could.

As Lucy and the friar parted from Peter at the door, Brother Simon turned, 'I confess the new learning, of which I had very little knowledge, well deserves to be called new.'

As King Charles had planned, a routine was established. Peter and Lucy had their traditional studies in the morning, most days they rode after the mid-day meal and then the experiments took place at William's shop.

Much to his relief, Peter seldom encountered the pages, save on those occasions that their paths crossed at the stables. When they did meet, Ferdinand le Gray and his closest friend, Richard Montague, spent a fair amount of time and effort in either trying to impress Lucy or mock Peter's manners. In the former activity they were not very successful.

'I find the pair of them most disagreeable, Peter,' she remarked. 'You have my permission to punch them next time they make fun of you.'

Peter nodded solemnly but refrained from telling her that his earlier attempt to do so had ended in a humiliating thrashing. It would be a little while before he would be a match for them.

Some two months after Peter's fifteenth birthday the king came into the schoolroom and announced that a Portuguese caravel had docked at the port and that he would like to take Peter to inspect it. Lucy begged to be allowed to come as well and the three set off down the steep hill to the quayside.

The lines of the little vessel astonished them. By comparison, the heavy ships of the traders and the Voravian warships looked slow and clumsy. The Portuguese captain was in the best of spirits; flattered by the attention his ship was receiving, and invited the Royal party aboard. They looked around the sleek craft.

The captain asked if Peter would like to go aloft and showed him the rope ladders on either side that led to the lookout point towards the top of the mast.

Peter had only climbed a short way when he began to feel a terrible sense of panic. He looked down and his head swam. He closed his eyes and gripped the rung with all his strength. Gradually his heart ceased to pound. He opened his eyes and focused on the next rung. 'Don't look down, just take each step at a time,' he told himself as he inched up. He lifted a foot that appeared to be as heavy as lead, up a rung. He took a deep breath and raised his other foot. He paused then moved one hand up.

'Come on Peter!' He heard a shout from the other ladder and, glancing nervously across, he saw Lucy, who appeared to have no fear of heights at all, fairly racing up.

At last, after a terrifying climb up an ever-narrowing ladder, Peter reached the crosstrees. He placed a hand on the mast and inched his way up and onto the boom that rested against it. Very slowly he straightened his back, fixing his gaze on the walls of

Nieuport high above them. By his side, and completely at ease, Lucy was waving down to her father.

Peter, his heart pounding, his chest tight with fear, turned to face Lucy and managed a strained smile.

Lucy turned to him, 'Really Peter! A big, tough, handsome boy like you shouldn't be put to shame by a mere girl. No. I'm being cruel. Lots of people have a great fear of heights. Just try to be brave. As brave as Belle,' she added, laughing. 'Now let's climb down.'

Peter closed his eyes and fought his terror. When he opened them he saw that Lucy had taken a masthead rope in her hands and was climbing down it hand over hand to the astonishment of the crew. She arrived at the deck, released the rope and made a deep curtsy to the captain before re-joining her father. Peter's descent was not as graceful. He first knelt on the boom and then groped with his foot for the first rung. Very, very cautiously he slid himself down until he had both feet safely on the ladder. He descended carefully, an enormous sense of relief flooding through him as every step brought him nearer to safety.

They returned to the palace, Lucy excitedly chatting to her father whilst Peter trudged along in their wake, overcome by his sense of failure and the very timid account he had given of himself.

That September Brother Simon announced that he had been summoned back to his monastery for six months. Both Peter and Lucy were sorry to see him go. His attitude to William's teaching had undergone a complete change. He was, by now, an enthusiastic follower of the new sciences. He assured his pupils he would return by the following spring.

The lessons with William continued in the friar's absence and one fine autumn day, as evening was starting to fall, Peter left the shop to escort Lucy back to the palace. They had only taken a few steps when a man holding the hand of a small girl accosted him. The man appeared to be blind.

'Excuse me, sir, I am trying to find the *Drum and Monkey* tavern in Trinity Street but my guide,' and here he indicated his small companion, 'doesn't know it. Could you perhaps show me where it is?'

'Of course, sir. Take my hand. The tavern's very close. It's just round the corner.'

All Peter had to do was to lead the man down a narrow passage opposite the shop and take two turns off it and they would be at the inn.

Leaving Lucy in the doorway of the shop, they crossed the road in front of a large cart pulled by two fine horses. Peter thought idly how unusual this was. Most carts were hauled by lumbering oxen. They entered the passage. About half way down they passed a small butcher's shop and Peter had to duck to avoid being hit by some pigeons that were hanging from above the shop front. The sight of the pigeons reminded him suddenly of the king's visit and the need to keep an eye on Lucy. He spun round. He could not see her. The cart had stopped, entirely blocking his view of his father's shop and Lucy. A wave of panic swept through him. He dropped the man's hand and pushed past him.

'Oi, what the hell are you doing?' the man shouted

and made a grab at Peter's tunic.

Peter shook himself free and began to run back up the passage, the man started out after him. The man who said he was blind.

Peter reached the street and darted round the back of the cart. Two men were approaching Lucy who seemed oblivious to any danger. Although the men wore the usual smocks of country farmers, their build and the way they walked gave a very different impression, that of professional soldiers.

Chapter 5

A TOLEDO BLADE

Peter reached Lucy just as one of them put out a hand towards her shoulder. He slammed a fist as hard as he could into the man's astonished face, threw open the door to the shop and bundled Lucy through it. He followed, and shot the bolt across.

Lucy, who had collided with the counter and slipped to the ground, pulled herself to her feet.

'What on earth was that about? Why did you hit that farmer?'

Peter stood leaning against the door panting.

'He was going to seize you. I'm sure he was.'

'Oh don't be ridiculous. Anyway I can look after myself. I'm no longer a child, you know.'

Peter said nothing. As his heart slowed from his exertion he began to wonder whether he had imagined the danger. Perhaps the first man had really been blind. Perhaps the farmer was really just that and had never meant to touch Lucy. He peeped out of the shutters. The cart had moved on though the man he had hit was still standing, nursing a bleeding nose and gazing at the door to the shop.

But there was, he knew, another reason he had reacted as he did. It was true. Lucy was no longer a child. Just as his body was rapidly changing, so was Lucy's. Hers was beginning to show the early signs of womanhood. Peter had accepted for a while that there had occurred an alteration in his feelings for her. No longer were they much the same as those he had felt for his other childhood friends. Now he longed for her company. He looked forward each day to seeing her, hearing her speak, watching the way she moved, even her scent. Above all, he wanted to protect her. Sunday, when there were no lessons and no Lucy, was now the worst day of the week.

He did not dare tell her any of this. He wondered whether she too felt anything similar for him.

King Charles summoned Peter to his study.

'Peter Salt, you are now sixteen and I've watched your progress these last four years. I believe you have all the qualities necessary to turn you into a knight of this realm. I know you are not highborn but then neither are many of my best knights. Indeed Sir Walter Martley, our nation's greatest soldier and a man I would trust with my life, came from a background a great deal more humble than yours. Since my existing squire has reached an age when he is ready to be a knight, I have decided to appoint you in his place. You may of course refuse this position but I would be most pleased if you were to accept.'

Peter was dumbfounded.

'Well, what do you say?'

'Sire, this is such an honour I…I cannot express my thanks.'

'Well then, don't bother. Come on, we must attend to your dress. You must look the part if you are to act the part.'

Peter paused. How could his parents afford the

sort of clothes a royal squire should wear?

'Sire, my father is a gentleman but he is not a wealthy man. I am afraid I shall have to decline the offer.'

'Peter, I owe your father much more than a few doublets, a few boots, a few capes and a suit of mail. I have asked my steward to arrange for my tailor to measure you for suitable garments and it will be a weight off my conscience to settle the account.'

Peter was about to salute and leave but he felt the king had not quite finished.

'A few moments ago I referred to Sir Walter, a man who - in the past - would never have risen beyond sergeant and there are others who have, by ability, prospered in modern Voravia. Now I have given you an opportunity many would believe unattainable, given your birth. My policy is not without its critics. Our nation won her independence by the efforts of a few brave and determined men. Their descendants, the nobility, have until recently held all the positions of power within the state. None of them tell me to my face that they resent the arrival of the new men. But of course they do. Whilst I am around men like Sir Walter will be safe to serve the interests of our country. I have often discussed my ideals with my daughter and I know the princess shares them, but I do fear what would happen were I to die before she reaches her maturity.'

There was another pause. Peter looked at his sovereign. He sensed, with a shock, the loneliness of a king's position. Behind King Charles' bluff good humour there lurked a sadness. He felt a great wave of sympathy and a fierce loyalty to his king. He was not sure whether he should say anything; then he plucked up courage. 'Sir, you entrusted the princess to my care when we were young. I will… I will die to protect her.'

'Well I hope it won't come to that. But I appreciate your words. Now, enough of this mournful mood. Off you go to the tailor and then I expect you'll want to break the news to your parents. I am away for a week or two. I like to see and be seen in all the corners of our land and I intend from now on to take Lucia with me. It will show our people there is a fine young woman to follow me.'

And so, a few weeks later, Peter presented himself to King Charles, who was seated at his desk in his study. Peter was dressed in a dark blue doublet with silver sewn collar, silver buttons and crimson leggings. Over this he wore a grey mantle similarly silver buttoned and a dark blue cap.

'Well, Squire Peter, you assuredly look very much the figure of a squire.'

The king paused then reached down and lifted a long piece of velvet. He laid it on the desk and carefully unwrapped the contents. Peter gazed at the object that was revealed. It was a sword. He knew at once where it had been made. The weapon had all the simplicity and perfect symmetry of a Toledo blade, the finest weapon a man could have. King Charles had given him, first, the most wonderful horse, and now this.

He looked up at the king who was now standing and laughing.

'Well, if you're to be at my side in battle, I'll be the happier to know you are suitably armed,' he joked.

Peter stretched forward a nervous hand and touched the hilt.

'Is this really for me to wear, sir? It's wonderful. It's… it's what I've always dreamed of fighting with.'

'Seems I've chosen a bit of a bloodthirsty young man,' the king admonished, but his eyes were twinkling, 'and yes, it's yours. See, I've had your initials engraved into the blade. Now let's see how it looks on you.' Peter sensed that the king was getting almost as much pleasure from the sword as he was.

Later that day Peter arrived at his parents' house, his sword at his waist. He could see that his mother was entranced by his appearance. His father, he suspected, thought that the money lavished upon such trifles as silver buttons could much more usefully have been spent on a hundred more worthy expenses. The sword was a different matter. Even William could see, at once, it was an exceptional piece of craftsmanship, an amalgam of practicality and elegance.

That evening, in the privacy of his bedroom, Peter took it lovingly from its simple leather scabbard. He held it gently and felt the comforting way the hilt embraced his hand and its perfect balance. He raised it vertically and gazed in awe at the honed silver-blue steel of the blade. A few thrusts at the wall and he was, in his imagination, a victor over insurmountable odds and a hero in Lucy's adoring eyes. He hung it from a peg, an object almost of reverence - his Toledo blade.

Peter was to look back at that moment as the one that confirmed his ambition to be a soldier.

The next day, King Charles called Peter to his study, complimented him again on his smart appearance and said, 'Peter, it will, of course, be necessary for you to live here at the palace with the other squires.'

A wave of panic swirled through him. He would be in close contact with Ferdinand. Although they had seen but little of each other during the past three years, the contempt that Ferdinand had for him, the jealousy arising from his close contact with the princess and the likely reaction to the deliberate smirk he had given him, would mean that Ferdinand would prove an undoubted tormentor.

For a second Peter thought about explaining this to the king but a moment's reflection led to his deciding that, if he were to fulfil his ambition to be a soldier, such a confession would not advance it.

He swallowed and replied. 'I understand, sire. I will go and explain the change to my parents.'

The king nodded and Peter left his presence.

Abigail bade a tearful farewell to her son.

'Remember, Peter, you are never far from my thoughts. Promise me you will nightly say your prayers and never forget that, as a Christian, you are always close to Our Lord and His saints.'

As he was only moving a few hundred yards, Peter felt she was being rather melodramatic. Nevertheless he assured her he would dutifully carry out the requirements of his faith

The following morning Peter dressed in his squire's uniform and strapped his sword to his waist. He walked up to the palace clutching a small bundle of belongings. He was very nervous.

Chapter 6

HENRY

Peter entered the ancient Harslanger keep. It was empty save for two servants and Peter spent an uncomfortable half-hour in the main hall, wondering which would be his room and what he should be doing. Eventually the main door swung open and a young squire entered carrying two large ledgers. Expecting either Ferdinand or one of the other young lords, he was mightily relieved that it was Henry Martley. Although they had not met before, Lucy had often spoken to him of Henry. She described him as a gentle, kind young man. He was, she had said with approval, quite unlike the rest of the boastful, arrogant noblemen who strode about the palace, with the confidence born of privilege.

'Why, Peter Salt, I'd heard that King Charles had asked you to become his squire and I'm sure he has made an excellent choice. Since there is a spare bed in my room I suggest you take it. I must warn you that you are likely to get a hard time from the other squires, as do I, on account of our not being born to titled families.'

Peter accepted the invitation immediately. He would need a friend and an ally. The room Henry showed Peter to was quite cramped and lit by a small window. As well as the two beds there were a couple of chests and a desk. The desk and the tops of the chests were littered with manuscripts. Henry made a half-hearted attempt to tidy the papers and opened one of the chests. On the wall was a shelf with four leather-bound books.

'They're poems. Over the years my mother has given them to me. I'm afraid I am not very much a man for swords and horses. My eyesight is not too good which may account for my lack of ability with a sword but, in truth, it's my temperament. I can appreciate better a well-constructed sonnet than a pacy gelding. I don't suppose you read much, but I'm sure we will get along. The princess tells me you are a decent sort of man.'

So that was the sum of the princess's feelings for him. Decent sort of man! Why could she not have described him as dangerous and exciting? Surely his fear of heights had not dropped him down so low in her opinion.

But, for the moment, he had other more pressing concerns.

'I've much to learn about the manners of the court. I'd be most grateful, Henry, really I would, if you'd help me. I'm bound to make the most appalling blunders. I somewhat dread having to live alongside le Gray.'

'I fear you're right to do so. He and his abetters haven't made my time here easy. He was sure he'd be appointed King Charles' squire. Indeed he boasted as much to the rest of us. So now he's embarrassed, and furious, not to get the post.'

'But surely he is indentured already?' Peter asked

'He is, to the Earl of Harford, but the earl is a

complete sot. He's drunk from dawn to dusk. Le Gray has applied to break his indenture. He will, I'm afraid, vent his disappointment on you. But, perhaps if we stick together, we can blunt his bullying.'

Peter looked at Henry then extended a hand. 'Henry, a harsh word or cruel act to either of us will be as to us both. I may be younger than le Gray, but I tell you, over the years I've probably had to use my fists more than he has. You can count on me.' Peter spoke these bold words with rather more confidence than he felt.

Although Henry was eighteen months older than Peter his slight frame and the fringe of black hair that flopped forward over his brow made him look younger than his years.

'Who are you squire to, Henry?'

'To the Earl of Bardsey. He's Voravia's Treasurer and responsible for the Royal finances. I may not be able to balance a sword or on a horse as well as Ferdinand and his lot, but I know how to balance a set of accounts. Not that such an ability counts for anything in the Harslanger.' Henry said this with a laugh and not a hint of bitterness. He would make an easy, good-natured companion.

That evening meal was the first time that Peter met the other six squires as equals. Ferdinand strode over to him. This was the man he knew he would daily have to confront. Although Ferdinand was the more heavily built, Peter was relieved to notice there was now little difference in their respective heights. Ferdinand's manner was haughty and contemptuous.

‘I’m told you’re King Charles’ new squire. I can hardly believe it.’

‘Yes, I am. I’m Peter Salt. I hope, Ferdinand, we can be friends.’

‘You have to be joking! You’ve had one thrashing from me, seems you’re going to need another pretty soon. God knows what King Charles must have been thinking of when he appointed you. Anyway, it shouldn’t take him long to regret his mistake. I hope you realise, Salt, that this is a place for nobility, not peasants like you or little milksops like spindle-shanks Martley with his poems and books. Hey, Martley, show Salt your latest drivel, he looks as if he could do with a bit of culture.’ Ferdinand gave Henry a sharp dig in his ribs.

Ferdinand’s insult was greeted with guffaws of laughter.

After breakfast the squires attended on their principals, Peter to the king, Henry to the Earl of Bardsey and Ferdinand to the befuddled Earl of Harford. Afternoons were devoted either to training in the skills required of a knight or recreation.

‘I am afraid I rather dread the afternoons,’ Henry confessed. ‘I do not show up very well at the physical activities and I am somewhat embarrassed at the lessons in tactics.’

On that first afternoon, it being a Wednesday, Sergeant Watts arrived to give instruction in swordsmanship.

‘Right, Master Salt, sir, you and Master Henry will be paired off.’ Watts handed each of them a wooden sword.

Henry had been right. Despite many months of instruction, he was no great swordsman. By the end of the session Peter found he could beat his friend.

'Master Henry, I 'ad 'oped that your 'aving a novice to fight would 'ave given you a bit more confidence.'

Henry shrugged the matter off with a laugh, somewhat to Sergeant Watts' annoyance.

Ferdinand, Richard and the other squires wore leather jacks, helmets and breastplates and used light steel swords.

On the Thursday the squires ascended to the roof of the Harslanger, the highest point in the castle, for a lesson in tactics from Sir Walter Martley, Henry's father.

'When he was fifteen my father was enlisted in the second war against Sloronia. After a few months he was appointed a sergeant. Then, during the siege of Gwestern, all the officers and over half the foot soldiers were killed in a stupid breakout. My father assumed command and held out for six months until King Charles led a force to relieve the castle. That was the start of his climb up the ranks.' Henry explained, omitting all details of his father's achievements in battle and organisation.

In complete contrast to his son, Sir Walter was a large, bluff, hearty man with a twinkling expression. Over his left eye he wore a patch. Peter wondered, with a shiver, what lay behind the piece of black leather. Did he remove it at night?

'Now, lads, if you remember one thing, let it be this, whilst tactics, bravery, physical strength and fine armour will help you in battle 'tis comradeship that will win the fight. It be my task to try to teach you to think wisely in the heat of warfare. That I will try to do, but comradeship be something only you can teach each other.'

Peter felt that behind Sir Walter's words was a plea to the squires to respect each other, and in particular, that they were addressed to those squires who were bullying his Henry.

Sir Walter spoke with a slow countryman's burr and used simple homespun language. Peter, with his military ambitions, listened attentively to the great general's advice, but the young nobles sniggered at his speech and took pleasure in imitating him once he had left. Peter guessed Henry found their behaviour most hurtful.

The Friday afternoon was devoted to the joust. Sir Lucian Astley - the great sportsman - supervised it. He was mounted on one of his magnificent horses.

'Lucian's father, Sir Hugh, is enormously rich and his stable is as fine as the royal one,' Henry explained. 'He's quartermaster to the army. Bardsey has never been able to explain quite how it is that the post of quartermaster seems to guarantee the holder a fortune.'

The squires, who laughed at Sir Walter, regarded Sir Lucian very differently. With his great wealth, fine horseflesh, skill in the lists and enthusiasm for the chase he was hero-worshipped by Ferdinand and his coterie.

Poor Henry hated the jousting.

'I can't think of a more ridiculous pastime. Not only am I useless at it, I have no desire to improve. I've had a word with Lucian and he has agreed to try to exempt me from it on account of my eyesight, but every so often I have to have a go.'

On that first afternoon Henry fell off twice before Peter's lance even made contact.

The next opponent was Richard Montague. Peter was determined to show those arrogant young nobles how well he and Belle understood each other. He lost the first course but won the next two. In the second, Montague fell heavily and sat shaken on the ground. Peter dismounted and went across to help him to his feet. Montague accepted a hand, but then turned his back on Peter and hobbled away.

Princess Lucia was often away from the castle now as the king took her about his kingdom. In her absence Peter's feelings seemed to grow more intense. It was absurd. Years ago he had learnt that she was destined for some foreign prince. Indeed it was worse. The man he most admired had expressly barred him from wooing her. It made no difference; she haunted his dreams.

An absorbing subject of the squires' conversation was chivalry; in particular each declared himself a champion of one of the ladies at court. Poor Henry, with his short sight, gentle disposition and incompetence at jousting was much mocked over whatever choice he made.

'It really does not matter who we squires decide to

champion, since no one has the courage to declare his ardour. I think I might as well choose the palace cat.' He paused then added, 'She'd probably not have me. I'd better choose the palace mouse.'

One afternoon, after a session at jousting, Ferdinand turned to Peter.

'And who do you fight for, apothecary?'

'The Princess Lucia.' Well why not? No one here knew of the king's embargo.

'You fight for the princess? You, the apothecary's son!' Ferdinand jeered. 'Just because she's had some stupid, boring lessons at your father's little shop doesn't give you the right to champion the princess. You should fight for someone from your own class, like Elspeth, her lady's-maid.'

This quip was greeted by roars of laughter from Ferdinand's followers who knew better than not to appreciate his humour.

Peter shrugged and then said, 'So be it. I fight for Elspeth. She will at least accept me as her champion.' He was not going to be drawn into a senseless dispute, one he could never win in practice. It would only torment him the more.

'Still, that's better than will o' the wisp, Martley here. No lady would accept a petticoat poet like him as a champion. Would they, my little scholar?'

Ferdinand strolled over to the table at which Henry had been seated writing. He snatched the small leather-bound book and began to disclaim the opening lines of a poem in a contemptuous voice. Then, walking to the window, he tossed the book out.

Henry looked up and spoke the next four or five lines. There was a short silence as the beauty of them affected all but the most malevolent of his oppressors.

'Piffle, never heard such rubbish! If your little notebook's ended up in the gutter below it's the best place for it, isn't it Richard?' Ferdinand threw his arm round Montague's shoulder.

'Ferdinand le Gray, you lay off Henry or you will have me to answer to,' Peter snapped. 'One more taunt, one more insult to a man with more talent in his little finger than you have in all your whole body and I'll smash that great boastful vain head of yours in.'

'My God, who's threatening who? Let me tell you, Salt, your days in this castle are numbered. You and I are likely to be enemies for the rest of our days here, and I can assure you of one thing, little apothecary, my days are likely to be a damn sight longer than yours. My father is the eleventh Earl of Greville. His was the tenth earl. Yours probably didn't even know who his was. There are many families like ours who think King Charles - good King though he most certainly is - has gone too far in promoting men from outside the nobility, those like Richard here and me, born and bred to govern. It can't be long before the king sees his experiment isn't going to work and then there will be a change back to the system that served our country so well all these years. When that change comes, Salt, you'll think yourself damn lucky if you are able to creep back, in one piece, to your disgusting little shop.'

Ferdinand reached for the bottle of claret and filled his fine silver goblet, etched with the Greville's crest of a shaggy, horned lion. He took a long pull on it

'It's true, Peter, the seventh Earl of Greville was one of our nation's greatest heroes. What I am trying to understand is how so little of that nobility has percolated down to his progeny,' Henry remarked mildly.

Le Gray appeared to be about to respond, but changed his mind, turned on his heel and left the room. A minute or two later, Peter went down into the court and found Henry's book. It had landed, not in the gutter, but had been caught up in the foliage of a climbing rose. He returned it to its owner.

A few days later, with a touch of frost in the sunny morning air, Peter set off with a couple of apples for Belle's stall. He nodded to a groom, who was attending to a lame horse in the yard, and entered the stable.

The next moment he received a heavy blow to the head that knocked him to the ground. For a moment he thought a stray horse had kicked him but, as he rolled over, he saw two of his fellow squires standing above him. Peter put his hand to his head. His hair felt sticky with blood.

He had been in fights before. At his school there had been disputes and many had been settled with fists. He crouched, trying to get his thoughts together. His opponents were Ferdinand le Gray and Richard Montague, Ferdinand's lickspittle. If he could beat le Gray, Montague would pose no threat, unless he could get behind him. Peter worked his way towards the wall of the stable.

'Well, little apothecary's son, think yourself mighty high and fine to be Princess Lucia's champion do you? I seem to recall you threatened me a while back, well now I'm going to ensure that never happens again.'

Le Gray stepped forward and swung his cudgel up and brought it down for a second blow to Peter's head, at the last moment Peter threw himself to his right and the stave glanced down his left arm. Peter felt a surge of pain as it ripped through his shirt and skin.

Chapter 7

THE NAIL

A hot flow of blood began to pour down towards his wrist. For a moment he thought his arm was broken, the pain was so excruciating. His right hand had landed in a pile of horse muck and, as he shifted it, he felt something hard and loose. It was a nail from a shoe. He grasped it in his fist. If he were going to have to fight for his life, any weapon would have to serve.

Montague stepped forward, drew off his left glove and turned the ring on his finger round, then smashed his palm into Peter's face, dragging his hand down. The stone sliced down Peter's cheek, almost cutting through to his mouth.

'Take that you jumped-up peasant,' he snarled and Peter caught the smell of wine on his breath.

They had been drinking. Perhaps he had a chance.

Peter lifted his shattered face. His right eye was closed. He could hardly make out his assailants.

Le Gray was leaning on his stave, smiling. He extended his left hand with his ring on it.

'If you value your life, promise me you'll resign your squiredom. Kneel before me and kiss my ring as a pledge of your word. As for being Lucy's champion, never even think about it, you cesspit worm. Get back to your shop.'

Peter moved forward on his knees. He bent his right knee and took the extended hand firmly in his left hand. He began to bend his head, then in a single movement he drew his head back and brought his right hand down with all his might onto the back of le Gray's hand. Peter felt the jar as the protruding point of the nail crunched into the bone and sinew. Le Gray gave a gasp of pain and surprise and dropped his club. The next moment Peter was up and facing him. He stamped with all his weight on le Gray's foot and, as le Gray stepped back, Peter, clutching the nail in his folded fist, hit him as hard as he could between the eyes. Peter was aware that a blow struck gripping something, even a piece of wood, is much less likely to damage the striker's fist. Even so there was a shock of pain through his knuckles. Le Gray must have been badly hurt. He raised his hands to his right eye and a trickle of blood ran down his nose.

'Help me, Richard,' le Gray shouted as Peter advanced on him.

Montague, appalled at the change in events, made a half-hearted lunge, trod in the horse muck, slipped and collided with le Gray. Peter seized his chance and brought his knee up into Montague's stomach. Montague gasped and then was sick, his vomit spewing over his friend.

'Urgh, you fool,' screamed le Gray. He tried to mop his face.

Peter stooped and picked up the stave. A fury such as he had never known raged through him. It was as if a red mist had filmed his eyes. Le Gray was off-guard, completely at his mercy. The flogging at their first meeting, the gibes at his lowly birth and the months of bullying of his friend Henry were about to be revenged, he would beat his enemy to a pulp. He swung the stave back aiming at le Gray's head. He was about to smash it down when he noticed Belle looking over her door. He paused. There seemed to be in her unblinking stare, a reproach. It was as if she were trying to tell her master she would not forgive his striking a defenceless foe.

He lowered the stave.

'Get out of here,' he whispered, 'get out before I really start on you.'

His two assailants stepped shamefacedly out into the yard. Peter tossed the stave back into the stable and followed them out. He staggered over to the wellhead.

A stable lad had just drawn up a pail of water and, when he saw the battered and bleeding Peter, he silently passed him the bucket.

Peter peeled off his shirt. His left arm was a mire of blood and bruising. He dipped a rag into the water and touched his wounds, flinching at the shock of the cold water. Slowly he began to clean up the raw flesh.

'What on earth has happened?' a voice cried out.

Peter looked up. Lucy, riding Tench, accompanied by Brother Simon on a grey palfrey and a stable lad leading King Charles' riding horse, Zephyr, had entered the yard.

Lucy's hand flew to her mouth when she saw Peter, his curls a bloody mass, his left eye closed, his face slashed open and his left arm hanging limply, with a great blue-black weal on his forearm suppurating blood.

'There's been a fight.' Peter mumbled.

'He attacked us, princess,' le Gray began.

'Really,' the princess replied with a toss of her head, 'I'm surprised he'd be so foolish, considering there were two of you. And you are both older. The injuries he's taken look very much as if it was not a very fair and chivalrous contest. What's more the pair of you don't seem to have given a very good account of yourselves since it is very evident to me who has won. Why are you boys so stupid? You shouldn't be fighting amongst yourselves, particularly when there are so much more urgent matters. King François of Sloronia crossed our frontier yesterday and we are at war. Papa, I mean the king, and I have just returned from visiting the Duke of Flanders and he has promised five thousand men-at-arms.'

The three boys looked at each other in surprise. Suddenly their little battle seemed irrelevant.

'I think you two should get back to your quarters now,' said Lucy. 'Peter, your face is in a terrible state. Brother Simon, could you see if you can do anything for it?'

Ferdinand turned on his heel and, still wiping the vomit from his face and tunic, made his way towards the Harslanger keep. Richard followed miserably behind.

They had gone but a few yards when Peter heard Ferdinand growl to Richard, 'You wait, you buffoon, 'til we get back to the room. I'll teach you a lesson you'll not forget.'

Peter took three rapid steps after le Gray and hissed in his ear. 'Le Gray, this matter is over. I could have killed you in there and you know it. Touch Richard or any of us just one more time and I'll show you how we street boys really fight. Understand?'

Le Gray turned towards Peter and said nothing. Peter seized le Gray's injured hand and slowly began to increase the pressure upon it. Le Gray gave a howl of pain.

'I asked you if you understood. Have the courtesy to let me have an answer.'

'Yes, yes, just let go,' le Gray gasped.

Peter eased his grip. Le Gray began to rub his hand. Then, giving Peter a look of hatred, he walked slowly towards the gate to the yard.

Brother Simon said, 'Now then, let's have a look at these injuries. The king has asked me to take charge of the wounded in the war that is to come, so I'd better get in some practice.'

As the friar gently tended Peter's wounds, Peter asked him why he had wished to go to the fighting.

'Like your father, Peter, mine wanted the best for me. He was a cobbler and a fine mender of boots but could neither read nor write. He sent me into the Church to get an education. But during these last twelve months, attending the princess's instruction at your father's house, I've become more and more interested in the study of anatomy. Did you know that your father has recently acquired a skeleton? I have begun to make a detailed examination of how the bones are put together. It shows the wondrous way of our Creator. One day I'd like to investigate the connection between our bones and our sinews. I have His Majesty to thank for my new absorption. In return I wish to serve him. I'm no fighting man, unlike you from what I see, but I hope to be able to offer something.'

'Brother Simon, the more I see of you the more I admire you. You're a fine man and a brave one. Let me shake your hand.'

Brother Simon gave Peter his hand and Peter noticed that the new confidence the friar had acquired was reflected in his much firmer handshake.

'That wound to your cheek will not mend on its own,' he said, shaking his head. 'I must stitch it up. Stay here. I'll go and get some thread.'

Peter sat on the wall to the well. Now that the fight was over he felt exhausted and began to shiver. It was not only the sweat evaporating from him, nor the danger he had been in, so much as the revelation of a side to his personality he did not recognise. He had been upon the point of killing his assailant and had felt a thrill at the prospect. A chance sight of his horse's troubled eye had stopped him. What would happen on a later occasion? He had heard about men who relished killing. Was he to become one of them? Was that why he had decided to become a soldier? Of one thing he was certain: his relationship with Ferdinand le Gray was one of mutual hatred. He would have to watch the man all the time.

Chapter 8

WAR

A stable boy came over.

'Reckon you give them two a good drubbing. You must be a fine fighter, young lad. Here, you look all in. Have my jacket.'

He took off a rough garment and draped it round Peter's shoulders.

When Brother Simon returned he had Princess Lucia with him, clutching a needle and silk thread.

Lucy asked, 'Peter what happened to you? They could have killed you. What was that about?'

'I really have no idea,' Peter replied. 'Something about women, I think.'

'You were fighting for your lady, were you Peter? How romantic, but a bit excessive do you not think?' She paused then added with the hint of a smile, 'And who is this lady you are prepared to have your tolerably good looks knocked about for?'

Peter was about to tell the princess that it was for her he had fought, then decided it would be better if he made a joke of the matter, 'Oh, 'twas Elspeth. But do not tell her. She's far too good for me.'

As soon as he said the words he regretted them. Would he ever get so good an opportunity to tell Lucy of his love? For that was what this feeling must be. This ache that was hurting him so much more than his battered body.

'Elspeth! Well, well, I had begun to hope that I,

your old school-friend, might be the object of your chivalry. But I suppose I'm not as pretty as Elspeth.' Lucy frowned then laughed, not very convincingly. 'I see I must try harder if I'm ever to be able to compete with my maid.'

Brother Simon threaded the needle and slowly drew the sides of Peter's wound together. Lucy watched, biting her lip. Peter glanced at her. Her worried expression surely indicated a concern for him, not just as a decent man but now perhaps as someone who would fight for … for Elspeth, he'd said. Oh what a fool he'd been.

'I'm afraid you'll carry that scar for the rest of your life.' The friar tied the last thread and stood up easing his back from the concentration.

'It will serve to remind you of the lovely Elspeth every time you look in your glass,' the princess teased. 'Brother Simon, you've done a neat job. The scar might even look rather manly one day. The Duke of Flanders arrives in two days' time so we must all look our best.'

'I've heard a lot about the duke,' Peter said, trying to be more cheerful. 'It seems he's a great fighter.'

'He and Papa are the oldest of friends. He has enormous estates and, come to think of it, he's probably much richer than Papa. He's got all those old-fashioned virtues of loyalty and courage that Papa says our modern generation no longer have. Mind you, his temper is a bit on the short side. Since he's a hard-riding, hard-fighting, impetuous man I expect you and he will get on splendidly. Although I believe he has a better head for heights,' Lucy added with a laugh.

Peter felt his heart jump with a rush of pleasure. Those teasing words were as sweet as any he had ever heard. All sense of pain evaporated. He walked up to the squires' quarters in a dream, reflecting on the contrariness of women. First, Lucy had admonished them for fighting, then had seemed to take quite a thrill in the thought of a fight over a lady.

As he opened the door he heard Ferdinand roar, 'Drink it, you numbskull. Drink my piss.'

Ferdinand had Richard pinned into a chair, with one hand squeezing his throat while with the other he was forcing a leather tankard to the squirming Montague's mouth. Montague was turning his head from side to side trying to avoid the foul liquid.

Peter strode forward. 'You heard what I said down in the yard, le Gray.' He seized the tankard and hurled its contents into le Gray's face.

'Richard Montague, my loathing and contempt for le Gray is such that, if he so much as lays one finger on you, I'll beat him to a bloody pulp. That's a promise.'

Montague looked with apprehension at le Gray then mumbled, 'Thank you, Salt. One day I'll repay you.'

Le Gray stood there mopping his face, his chest heaving with anger.

That evening Peter attended the king. He had made an effort to appear as smart as he could but there was no disguising his stitched cheek and a great swollen bruise over a black eye.

King Charles was at his desk with a mountain of documents before him and his seal of state at his elbow. He looked up and Peter felt the man had aged almost overnight. Once again he felt that surge of loyalty. The king was wearing a pair of spectacles, which he removed to rub his tired eyes. The room was brightly lit with candles and two young clerks, both in clerical garb, sat at small desks penning more documents with scratchy quills.

'It's the paperwork not the fighting that I find so exhausting when we go to war. And speaking of fighting, it looks as if you have started a bit early. I gather there was some sort of trouble in the stable yard this afternoon. Well, it seems you have survived and rumour has it you won. Don't bother to explain. There are few secrets within these walls. Your young body will soon mend.' King Charles paused as if in memory of the past, then he went on, 'What it is to be young! Have a few scuffles, kiss a few girls, drink a few rounds and go to bed without a care in the world to sleep like a baby. Make the most of it, Peter. The years gather pace as we grow older. Soon you'll be like me, nothing more than a clerk. Oh, I meant no disrespect.' He turned to his two assistants, who, Peter could not help thinking, had had very few scuffles, if that was what King Charles called a fight to the death, and not kissed too many girls. 'Now let me see. This pile is to go to the Earl of Bardsey. He will act as purser for the duration of the war.' The king indicated a stack on one side of his desk. 'I don't know what I'd do without the earl. He seems to get as much pleasure out of a set of balanced books as I do from hearing a piece of music well played.' He shook his head in disbelief.

The arrival of the Duke of Flanders brought a great stir to the castle. His entourage trotted up to the main gateway. His soldiers made camp on the meadows along the riverbank. In the event, his promised five thousand turned out to be no more than three thousand. As Henry Martley remarked, such is so often the way with promises given at short notice.

Peter, in attendance on the king, watched as the duke, a small wiry aristocrat with a weather-beaten face, greeted the king with great good humour. The king clapped him on the back, called up a bumper of claret, and led him into the royal apartments. Childhood friends, they made an odd pair; the big slow-moving king and the fiery little duke, like a mastiff and a terrier.

The next day Sir Walter Martley brought a company of archers and foot soldiers from his much smaller estates.

When all was ready King Charles summoned his generals, captains and knights, all attended by their squires, to the main courtyard and addressed them.

'Citizens and comrades, we have never desired anything save peace and friendship with our neighbours. Yet King François, ever anxious to annex Voravia, has torn up the treaty we signed but five years ago and invaded our sovereign lands. He has seized our castles at Forforn and Gwestern. He has chosen to attack us and we must show him how Voravia responds to any attack upon our territories. Tomorrow we march to give him battle. My half-brother, Prince Rupert of Heinz-Coburg, with his contingent will join us at the bridge over the river Mintz. That bridge, gentlemen, is the first objective of our advance.'

Peter learnt that by calling on other lesser nobles and gentry, the king would have almost six thousand men at his disposal in addition to about five hundred knights and some two hundred freelance horsemen.

The next day the army attended a solemn mass at which Archbishop Godwin, having invoked the Almighty's aid, assured the troops that they were fighting for a just cause. Then the army set forth.

The day was a beautiful late autumn one. The ladies of the court, dressed in their finest silks, watched the departure of the knights on their proud horses, their young squires in attendance, and the archers and pikemen in good spirits thanks to an advance of pay. Peter noted with surprise that in addition to their army-issued weapons, many carried at their waists private ones, cudgels, daggers and, in a few cases, swords.

The road they were following led for the first few miles across a landscape of farms and woods. The sun bathed the trees in reds and golds. By the time the army made camp for the night they had reached the Vesterdorpf Wolds. The wooded countryside had given way to open chalky downland with springy turf underfoot. Peter rode beside Henry Martley. He felt a tremendous sense of excitement and adventure. A feeling not far removed from immortality was surging through him as he looked across at his friend. Henry's slight frame looked very vulnerable now they were riding to war. The lock of black hair fell down his brow and his dark eyes had a faraway look to them. Unlike Peter, who was in the best of moods, the young poet seemed to be consumed with doubts.

'Well, this is more like it. I'm quite looking forward to the fighting. I just hope Belle won't get hurt.'

Henry turned an unusually serious face to him.

'This is how all wars start. With trumpets, cheers and banners flying bravely. I'm afraid they usually end with deaths, wounds, tears and grieving womenfolk. Look at these foot soldiers. They should be ploughing their fields instead of marching to war. My lord, the Earl of Bardsey, who is no soldier but understands the new science of economics, says all wars start after a good harvest. The barns and the treasury are full. If you want peace, pray for a crop failure. I suppose it ill becomes me to criticise the business of war seeing that, were it not for my father's military skills, both he and I would have a life of drudgery in the fields, but, for every Sir Walter Martley, there are hundreds of lives shattered by war.'

Peter tried to think of a counter-argument but, as so often in discussion with Henry, he felt he had already lost.

'But,' Henry added, his face now its normal smiling self, 'let us at least enjoy the glorious beginnings. Come on, these uplands are the finest riding country you could ask for. I'll race you to the front of the column. You'll have to give me a start. That mare of yours is a real flyer.'

Peter allowed Henry about a hundred yards then let Belle go. He received the accustomed thrill at her acceleration and the exhilaration of her speed as they swept past the trudging men. As he closed on Henry, he eased Belle off and Henry reached the head of the column first and turned a delighted face to Peter.

'Next time we start level. You're becoming too good a horseman, Henry,' Peter panted, giving Belle a stroke and a pat on her steaming neck.

During the pause for the midday meal, taken under the lee of an ancient hill-top fort, a young freelance officer came across. He was dressed in tawdry finery; up close his brocaded jerkin was soiled and threadbare. He was called Knud, came from Sweden and spoke barely a word of Voravian. It was Peter's Toledo blade that had drawn him over. Peter handed it to him. Knud examined it with a professional eye. He could not have been more than two or three years older than Peter yet behind his startling blue eyes there appeared to be a weary void. It was as if his young body were but a husk, his soul having been sucked out of him by a life of random killing. Knud returned the sword with a bow and a thin smile and sauntered back to his colleagues.

'Thinking of joining 'em when this is over? You wouldn't be the first lad to reckon it'd be a fine adventurous life.' It was Sergeant Ben Watts, his old instructor.

Peter laughed and shrugged.

'They be the sweeping of the gutters; criminals and fugitives. Spend all their wages at the tavern or brothel or in wagering. Not the sort of company for a decent Christian lad like you.'

'And the officers?'

'Worse if you ask me. Their only loyalty is to themselves. Discipline's maintained by the coin or the lash. Mostly the lash. Five years ago we 'ad another lot, Company of the Star, they was. There were a fight over something in a tavern and three of 'em got stabbed. Did their officers do anything about it? Did they hell! That ain't the way to run an army. Don't suppose this here Company of the Fang are any better.'

For two days the column pressed forward through the smiling landscape. Each evening the army halted, fires were lit, meat and game cooked and a ration of silverbrord and ale served. Friendships between strangers sprang up and all the camaraderie of army life started to develop. Peter and the squires trotted up and down the line bearing messages. The grandest nobles had two horses, a light, sprightly one for the march and a great heavy warhorse capable of carrying a fully armoured knight. The warhorses would be led on a rein by their squire or a stable lad. Peter often had charge of King Charles' Stang, who slouched along like a fighter conserving his energy. At the rear of the column came the packhorses carrying the heavy steel armour of the knights and behind them, a score of carts hauled by oxen. This was the baggage train and the army moved at its slow plodding pace.

On the morning of the fourth day they breasted a slight rise in the ground and below them appeared a wide, cultivated valley. A line of trees marked the course of the river Mintz and somewhere within the trees was the bridge.

The Sloronians had originally crossed the river but King Charles' scouts had reported that they had withdrawn to a better position on the far bank. Sir Walter's opinion was that the original invasion had been designed to goad King Charles into attacking. If so it had succeeded.

King Charles called a council of war. 'Prince Rupert is to meet us here and we could wait for him, but I would prefer to know that the bridge was secure. Flanders, would you be so good as to take a small party down there and, if the way is clear, hold the bridge until the main body arrives? Take three or four squires. It will give them some excitement. Send a couple back once the bridge is held.'

The duke set off with ten knights and Ferdinand, Richard and Peter. This was the first time since the fight in the stable that Peter had come across Ferdinand. Le Gray was an impressive sight in his fine chain mail with the Earl of Harford's tabard. He gave Peter a long, hard stare that showed a mix of arrogance and hatred.

The little party trotted down the track. Then the duke kicked his stallion into a gallop and, in high spirits, the others followed. They reached the valley floor and careered through farms and copses very much as if on a hunt. Peter tapped Belle on her withers and she responded by passing the rest of the party until they were level with the duke.

The tough little nobleman turned and gave Peter a grin.

'This is more like it, eh? When I was your age, I recall how bored I became on those interminable marches that always seem to precede the action. Can't say I care for them much even now.'

They rounded a bend and there was the bridge. A hail of bolts from crossbows greeted them. The duke's horse caught one and went down, as did those of four other knights.

Chapter 9

THE BRIDGE

Peter yanked on his left rein and managed to swerve into a small copse. He pulled up, gasping for breath.

The duke was staggering to his feet, cursing and swearing. A second volley felled four of the knights and Richard's horse.

The survivors regrouped in the woodland. The duke was horseless and in a furious temper. He drew his sword and demanded an immediate assault on the enemy. The remnants of the force drew their weapons but a good deal less enthusiastically. There were six knights, all very lightly armoured in chain mail, and three squires none of whom had ever been in battle. They had only eight horses between them.

One of the knights, Sir Gerard de Vere, suggested that he should go forward and reconnoitre the size of the defending force. The duke was at first inclined to press on with his assault but the futility of it gradually dawned upon him and he agreed to Sir Gerard's plan.

'Take those three squires, might as well use 'em. Send one back when you reach the river to let me know you've got there safely, then another with your report.'

Peter, Ferdinand and Richard joined Sir Gerard on foot and they set off through the undergrowth.

They were making for a spot about fifty yards

downstream from the bridge. Peter arrived first, slipped down the bank and began to inch himself forward towards the bridge.

From behind him he heard Sir Gerard tell Richard to return with the news that they had reached their first objective. The recent dry spell meant that the water was quite shallow and large expanses of caked mud lay between it and the banks. He was hidden from the men on the bridge by a bend in the river and managed to get within twenty feet of his objective. He peered round the corner. The bridge, an ancient stone structure with a small gatehouse at one end, was held by about thirty men armed with crossbows and backed up by five or six mounted knights.

As he turned round and began to make his way back, he heard shouts and the clash of swords from the direction of Sir Gerard and Ferdinand. Nervously Peter drew his Toledo blade. He hurried back. The thick vegetation that overhung the banks of the river made for slow progress but eventually he reached the spot where he had left Sir Gerard and Ferdinand. There was no one there. He paused and listened. There were only the drowsy sounds of autumn. A peacock butterfly floated among the nettles. He crept round the next bend and saw, lying face down in the water, the body of Sir Gerard and, on the opposite bank, two Sloronian knights pulling a fallen comrade from the waters.

Peter stopped in horror. The current was tugging at Sir Gerard's body so that it appeared to be stirring but Peter was almost certain the knight was dead.

As he bent down to try to turn the body over, he heard a slight movement behind him and spun round. Two armed men were standing in the bushes. One had his sword drawn.

'Well, who have we here?' the taller one asked in the distinctive Sloronian accent.

Peter stopped. He was hopelessly outnumbered. One of the knights on the far shore was already beginning to wade across. There was no sign of Ferdinand. He racked his brains to recall Sir Walter's instructions. *'There is all the world of difference between a reconnaissance patrol and a fighting patrol. The object of the first is to give the commander the information he needs to plan his strategy. The object of the second is to disrupt the enemy's actions.'*

Both the duke's patrol and Sir Gerard's were surely reconnaissance ones. He must get back with his information. He must avoid the fight, which he was bound to lose. For a second he wondered whether he was showing cowardice. Should he take on these three foes and die a noble death, a hero in Lucy's eyes forever? It briefly occurred to him that she would never know the circumstances anyway.

Peter had one advantage over his enemies, he was lightly armoured whereas they were in their breastplates and helmets. If he could get up the bank and into the trees he might be able to outrun them. He sheathed his sword and ran upstream on the dried mud, looking for a place to climb the bank. He could hear the soldiers above him struggling through the undergrowth. He came to a tree whose roots had been undermined by the spates of the previous winter and had slipped into the river. He scrambled up onto it and clambered onto the bank

His pursuers were about twenty yards to his left. Peter began to creep as silently as he could away from the river. After about ten minutes the vegetation thinned out and he emerged into an area of open cultivated land.

A flash of sunlight on steel over towards a copse on his left caught his attention. He screwed his eyes up and was just able to make out a group of men. He presumed them to be the duke's party.

Peter set out at a jog towards them. The sun beat down and the humid afternoon air was thick with drifting seeds. The sweat streamed down his face and at every step his sword thumped his calf painfully. As he ran he became more and more worried that his actions had been ignoble. At last, exhausted, he arrived at the copse. Ferdinand was standing beside the duke. He appeared to be nursing a wound on his arm.

'Well, where have you been?' the irascible duke barked at Peter.

'You don't need to ask him that, your grace.' Ferdinand spoke calmly. 'As soon as we were attacked, he fled. Hasn't got the guts of a house mouse.'

Peter stood there panting for breath. Then he managed to gasp out, 'The bridge is held by about thirty-five men including five or six knights.'

The duke ordered a withdrawal.

They had barely been gone thirty minutes when

round the corner ahead of them appeared a body of men. The leading figure, the Prince of Heinz-Coburg, was dressed in a fine suit of chain with a tabard of a black dog on a gold background across his chest. He was supported by a squire bearing a standard with the same badge and the motto *Cave Canem*. The prince's dark, handsome face was narrow and haughty. Above his full lips he sported a fashionable thin moustache. Behind him trotted thirty or more knights all finely apparelled and behind them a large number of foot soldiers.

Peter, exhausted, shaking from his run and aware that his actions were appearing in an ever worse light, could not but notice that Prince Rupert's squire cut a far more fashionable figure than he, the king's one, did. Not only was his over-tunic beautifully woven but around his neck, on a gold collar of intertwined Hs and Cs, hung a jewel-encrusted medallion comprising a black hound and the prince's motto.

'Well, well, Flanders, you look as if you've met your match,' the prince called out. Peter thought he detected, in the prince's tone, a hint of pleasure.

'Rupert, regrettably you are right. The bridge is held. We've lost Sir Gerard de Vere and my horse has taken a bolt. We were not sufficiently armed for their numbers. We were on our way back to bring up the army.'

'How many hold the bridge?' the prince enquired.

'Thirty bowmen and six knights,' the duke said. 'Should be no match for your lot.'

The prince paused to consider the situation then turned to one of his companions.

'Sir Robert, take that bridge,' he ordered. 'Any of you squires have a horse?'

Ferdinand, still ostentatiously displaying what Peter believed to be a very light wound, stepped forward.

'What's your name, squire? Are you able to ride or is your wound too severe?'

'I'm Ferdinand le Gray, sire, son of the Earl of Lowers. Although my wound is quite painful I shall be happy to convey any message.' Ferdinand was relishing the opportunity to display his bravery and usefulness.

'Thank you, le Gray. I know your people well. Among the best in our land. I appreciate your attitude. You seem to have acquitted yourself rather better than the rest of the duke's men. I will send my squire back with you. Collect your mount and ride back to King Charles and inform him that Flanders' plan failed but that, by the time he brings his force down here, the bridge will be secure.'

Ferdinand, with a show of discomfort, mounted and, with a small half-smile towards Peter, set off for the king, doubtless with the intention of not only conveying the Prince's message but also reporting that Peter had deserted Sir Gerard.

When, that evening, the main force arrived at the bridge it was now in safe hands. It would appear that on seeing Sir Robert's substantial force the Sloronians had withdrawn. The Duke of Flanders, who had been forced to watch its capture, was in the worst of moods. Peter, realising that the patrol had achieved nothing, as the bridge would have been taken by Prince Rupert's force in any event, was in total dejection.

King Charles' steward sought out Peter and ordered him to attend the king that evening when camp had been pitched.

'Ferdinand is putting it about that you deserted Sir Gerard when the Sloronians attacked your party. I know it cannot be true,' Henry told him

'No, it's not true. Really, Henry, I give you my word, it's not.'

It was with a dreadful sense of foreboding that Peter washed himself carefully, donned his best attire, fastened his sword to his belt and approached the royal pavilion.

Chapter 10

DISGRACE

The Steward met him and showed him into the king's presence. To his left was the duke. To his right, his face a studied mask of solemnity, stood Ferdinand le Gray. King Charles looked up. His jaw was set, he spoke coldly.

'I am informed that during the fiasco at the bridge you deserted Sir Gerard de Vere thereby leaving him and Ferdinand le Gray to fight a hopeless battle. If there is any truth in this report it shows appalling cowardice and you will, at best, be immediately stripped of your rank of squire and serve as a common soldier. At worst you will be put to death in front of the entire army at tomorrow's dawn parade.'

Peter swallowed. His mouth was as dry as tinder, his heart thumping, he had never been so terrified before, even when up the mast of the Portuguese man-of-war.

'Sir, I did not desert Sir Gerard. I went forward to scout the bridge and when I returned Sir Gerard was dead.'

'And did Sir Gerard order you to leave him?' the king asked.

'No, not in so many words, but I....I knew that was what we were to do. So as soon as we reached the river I went forward. I expected the others to be with me. I did not turn to see if they were. I was so concerned to keep out of sight from the enemy.' He was fighting for his life.

'So you took it upon yourself to carry out a reconnaissance patrol without an order from your superior officer and in doing so you led to a brave knight's death.'

Peter could only dumbly nod his head. To his horror he felt the tears begin to sting his eyes. He gritted his teeth. His breath was coming in short gasps from his heaving chest.

King Charles sat in thought for a few seconds. 'You will remove your insignia of rank. You will hand your horse over to the Master of Horse and you will report to Sergeant Schmidt forthwith. You may count yourself very fortunate to have escaped with your life. I am conscious of my debt to your father. In sparing your life I feel I have repaid it in full. I must take some responsibility for misjudging you as a man. You were unworthy of the status of squire, let alone that of a knight. You are dismissed from my presence.'

Thunderstruck, Peter saluted the king, who had turned to a sheaf of papers, and left the tent. The king's steward received his tabard and epaulettes. A common soldier, he stumbled back towards Belle and the encamped army. As he did so le Gray caught up with him.

'First whiff of action and what do you do? Skulk off to save your precious dirty little tradesman's skin, hey? Well, looks like you'll have to mix with your own sorts from now on. Though, come to think of it, those tough farm lads may want to knock some of the airs and graces off your cowardly little hide. But there is always a silver lining to any disappointment. You will have learnt a lesson that will serve you well for the rest of your humdrum little life. So don't forget. Don't try to mix on equal terms with the likes of me or others from my class. Oh, I nearly forgot. I doubt even a little slut like Elspeth will have much time for a man reduced to the ranks for abject cowardice.'

Peter took a step forward.

'Oh, don't even think of using your fists. Striking an officer is a capital offence. One blow and you'll swing for it. There is a vacancy now as King Charles' squire. I think I'll apply. Harford is a stupid drunken old fool. He needs a nursemaid not a squire. He can manage without me.' Ferdinand was in excellent spirits.

Peter began to make his way towards Sergeant Schmidt's platoon. He felt utterly crushed. He knew that cowardice was the soldier's worst crime. He was an outcast, hated and despised by all. Even his body now felt in tune with his mood. His arm ached and throbbed, his stitched cheek snagged on his teeth. All around him soldiers were at their tasks or resting in the sun. There were cheerful laughs and the genial comradeship of an all-male society. It was all in complete contrast to his misery. He felt, for the first time since his early schooldays, that very masculine longing for the gentleness of a woman to sooth his broken body and spirit.

Sergeant Schmidt was a short bull of a man whose head and neck seemed all one. Word had reached him that he was to receive a new man into his platoon, a disgraced former squire. He had no intention of giving a coward a warm welcome.

'So you're Salt are ye? Well, you'd better find a place to stow your stuff but don't expect any of my lads to make a space for you beside 'em. They're a brave lot. Ye'd not catch one of them turning tail. Then you can start digging the latrines, just the sort of job for a lousy little funk.'

The dreadful day continued as it had started. The men in the platoon, conscripted farm labourers, either shunned him or took every opportunity to barge him to one side. Under a blistering sun he, together with a soldier on punishment, dug a trench into the baked earth. Eventually Sergeant Schmidt arrived to inspect it and promptly told them to fill it in and start again. By evening Peter was exhausted, his hands blistered and raw.

'You're on guard tonight, Salt and if I catch you sleeping, you're for it.'

Peter lined up to draw his rations, feeling conspicuous in his fine, but now sweat-soaked, clothes amid the simple smocks and jerkins of the other men. The issue was of the plainest sort, a lump of stale bread and a badly cooked piece of gristle from some scrawny goat and a slice of inferior silverbrord. He took his food over to a bank and ate in lonely silence.

As night fell, fires were lit and the men began to sing and joke as they prepared for sleep beneath the stars. The guards were posted around the camp.

Peter was close to the lines for the horses and in the dark he could hear them stir. Somewhere among them was Belle. He would never ride her again. Now in the privacy of the dark he let the tears run down his cheeks. Within a space of a day he had fallen from being the king's squire with a wonderful mare, a good friend of Henry Martley, and the prospect of a promising military career to a despised foot soldier with no future whatsoever. Into his mind swum the laughing face of Lucy as she teased him about his fear of heights. His very heart was broken.

Behind him the fires began to settle, the voices trailed away. A terrible weariness crept up over him. What would he give for a few hours of welcome sleep?

He got up and began to pace up and down, more so as to keep himself awake than to patrol his beat. As he did so he recalled his mother's words to him. He was in her thoughts always. Once again he felt the sting of tears in his eyes. Then her second remark, that he was ever close to His Lord. He had not said his prayers each night as he had promised her, but now he found himself turning to his faith. As he did so, the story of Christ's awful vigil in the garden of Gethsemane came into his mind. He had heard the story so many times at Easter. In the Salts' family church, there was a fresco depicting the event. But now, for the first time, he fully understood the terrible loneliness Christ must have felt as He waited for His agonizing death. Then, as Peter contemplated an experience even worse than his own, he felt a slow lightening of spirit. No longer were his thoughts entirely self-centred. It was quite easy to ask for God's help. He wanted no miracle, just that, if given an opportunity, he would prove himself worthy. He would fight his way out of his troubles.

Within the camp the fires were just tiny glowing embers, there was no moon and beneath the trees it was pitch dark. Then Peter heard something. It was the softest of sounds. Perhaps it was just an animal. He stopped his pacing and stepped into the shadows. The sound came again. It was too stealthy for an animal. There was someone or perhaps more than one person just a little way into the trees. He listened intently. Then he heard another sound, much louder and more purposeful, coming from the direction of the camp. He peered in its direction and saw Sergeant Schmidt approaching. Peter waited in the dark until the sergeant was almost level with him then stepped out and saluted.

'Salt, what are you playing at? You scared me out of my wits.'

'There's someone out there,' Peter whispered urgently into the little sergeant's ear.

Although Peter was but a common soldier, his tone carried the authority of his training and Schmidt allowed himself to be steered into the shadow of the trees.

The two of them waited. There was total silence, then Peter heard the faintest of rustles, followed by a slight cough and a 'shh'.

Peter silently drew his sword. Sergeant Schmidt unhitched a cudgel from his belt.

They waited. Peter felt his heart pounding with excitement. Then he saw five, no six, men begin to creep across the open ground towards the horses. This must be a Sloronian cutting-out party intent on disrupting the Voravian advance by removing as many horses as possible.

Peter looked at Schmidt for an order. He was not going to make the same mistake as at the brook. The sergeant seemed to be cowering further and further back into the shadows.

'Shall we attack now?' Peter whispered. He was thinking fast what Sir Walter had taught about ambushes.

Schmidt turned a face contorted with fear towards Peter.

'I'll creep in behind them. Give me a two-minute start. Then you rush at them, shouting. They'll panic.' Schmidt nodded. He was shaking with terror.

'Don't worry, it'll be fine.' Peter mouthed the words in the sergeant's ear. He slipped away towards the spot the Sloronians had come from. As he did so, he recalled Sergeant Watts' advice, '*When fighting a man without armour, go for his legs. If he can't stand, he can't fight.*'

He reached a slight path through the undergrowth and paused. He could see the enemy grouping, ready to attack the horses. The seconds slipped by. What was Schmidt thinking of?

Then he heard a hoarse shout and Schmidt emerged waving his cudgel in a most un-warlike manner. He took a few steps towards the Sloronians and paused.

‘Go on, scare them!’ Peter was speaking under his breath. But Schmidt had started to withdraw. There was nothing for it. He would have to attack without the benefit of surprise. Peter, his sword in his hand, strode towards the cutting-out party. There were six of them, only lightly protected with leather tunics. He singled out the apparent leader and cut him to the ground; a second blow felled another. The remaining four started to engage Peter in a none too enthusiastic skirmish but their weapons were only daggers and short swords and were no match for a Toledo blade handled after months of practice. First one withdrew with a blow to the thigh, then the rest turned tail and ran. Peter was after them and managed to catch one more. He stopped his chase and turned back towards the horse lines. Sergeant Schmidt was beating the first of the fallen Sloronians to death with his cudgel.

Peter was just restraining Schmidt from dealing with the second wounded man in like manner when he looked up to find that Richard Montague, who was the officer of the watch, had arrived with the duty platoon.

‘We caught them raiders, sir. Trying to steal the ’orses they were.’ Schmidt was panting from his exertions and quick to take the credit.

‘Well done, sergeant. I’ll manage from now on.’

‘There’s another one in here, sir.’ Peter volunteered, pointing into the undergrowth.

He stepped into the bushes followed by Richard and four or five others. They quickly came across the injured soldier.

As they were carrying the two wounded men back to the camp, Peter heard one, the commander of the cutting-out party, say to Richard, 'We ain't come out of this too well, sir. We was beaten by just one of your lot.'

'Oh were you? I will inform the general. The sergeant here will get his reward.'

'No, it weren't him. Never saw him do no fighting,' the man replied in a tone of contempt. 'It were yon lad with 'is sword. We could do with a few the likes of him.'

The camp, when they reached it, was astir with news of the attack on the horses and its repulse. A crowd soon gathered around the victorious party. Schmidt, anxious no doubt to avoid too much of an enquiry into his part in the fight, now chose to heap praise on Peter.

'We made a grand team, we did. Young Salt showed a lot of pluck. I could never have managed things without 'im.'

Richard Montague came up to Peter. 'I gave my word to you and I intend to keep it. I saw what happened at the river. I know you didn't run away. When Sir Walter dismisses the watch at reveille, I shall tell him the truth. Well fought and ... and good night.'

He was about to leave when he turned round and said, 'Peter Salt, I behaved atrociously to you in the stable, can you forgive me?'

Peter offered a hand.

'The princess says my scar might look quite heroic

one day. Anyway, I expect we will all of us take a few cuts and bruises by the end of this campaign. Forget the incident. I have. And thanks for undertaking to help me.'

Chapter 11

A DREADFUL DISCOVERY

Sergeant Schmidt invited Peter to share a bumper of wine in his tent. Schmidt drank far too much and Peter became more and more embarrassed by the man's repeated and ingratiating assurances that they made a fine team. At last the sergeant fell into a deep sleep with resounding snores and Peter was able to slip away and settle down. His sleep was punctuated by nightmares, no doubt brought on by the events of the previous day.

He was woken early by the king's steward, who was carrying his tabard and epaulettes.

'His Majesty requests your attendance at his pavilion immediately,' the man said with a smile.

'I'm filthy. I must wash.'

'Oh, I doubt the king will mind. In fact his mood is such that I think he will be amused.'

King Charles rose as Peter entered. He extended a hand.

'I don't know who has been the more miserable this last day and night. When Sir Walter told me that Montague had been to see him and reported that you were not present when Sir Gerard was attacked, I felt an enormous sense of relief. I understand you showed not inconsiderable bravery last night. The news of your pluck will be all around the army by now. Some years ago I told your father that people think me over-hasty, impetuous you might say, and yesterday I did act too precipitously. But perhaps no harm has been done. I have learnt how much I enjoy your company and I am sure you've learnt much of value. Now, let us return to our former relationship. Go and smarten yourself up, collect your horse and report to me for breakfast with my generals within the hour. Your attendance will advertise your return to my service as squire. The advance can wait a few hours.' He paused then added, 'I think you will be more comfortable if you invite a friend.'

Peter bowed. He was speechless with relief. He considered inviting Richard Montague, whose courage in reporting the truth of the events at Mintz had saved him. But he was hardly a friend. He would thank him when they next met. He would ask Henry.

Peter was seated beside General Sir Forde Gryston. Neither he nor Henry said much at the meal, the company being so grand. Although everyone was polite to them, they were relieved when the meal ended and they were able to slip away to their duties.

As they left the king's pavilion Peter turned to Henry. 'I know I've been absolved of deserting Sir Gerard but I am still haunted by my reactions when I found his body. I didn't know what to do. I could have fought his killers and perhaps I would have won. In my imagination I fought all three and killed them all. But I did not. What should I have done, Henry? The purpose of our patrol was to find out how well the bridge was held. Surely I did the right thing even if it was not too…too glorious?' Peter looked nervously at his friend.

'Of course you did.' Henry's reply was quick, perhaps too quick.

Then he added. 'Peter, would you mind if I told my father how worried you are? After all, it was thanks to his instructions in tactics you acted as you did.'

Peter was about to tell Henry not to bother when Henry remarked, 'Incidentally, how come Ferdinand was back with the duke when you got there? I'll wager he deserted Sir Gerard, and by blaming you, he has managed to hide his own cowardice.'

'You could be right, Henry. But although Ferdinand is a horrible man, I've never thought him a coward. Now I must find Richard. He was as good as his word in reporting the truth about what happened in the river. I must say I feared he would be too frightened of le Gray to do so. I quite expected him to change his mind.'

Peter looked around but Montague was nowhere to be found. He came across Prince Rupert's squire and asked if he had seen Richard.

'Yes, but not recently. I saw him in the company of Ferdinand le Gray shortly after reveille. They were leaving the camp.'

'On foot? They cannot have gone far.'

'No, they were mounted. There seemed to be some sort of argument in progress.'

That evening a terrible discovery was made. The body of Richard Montague was discovered hanging from the branch of a tree. His horse was grazing a few yards away. Brother Simon, who prepared the body for burial, reported that it appeared he had received a blow to the head probably caused by his swinging into the trunk of the tree. His friend, Ferdinand le Gray, said that when he parted from Montague he seemed depressed and homesick.

Richard's suicide cast a sense of sorrow over all the young squires.

Chapter 12

GREENSLEEVES

By noon on the following day the leading scouts had reported that King François had drawn up his men at the top of a steep rise about three miles away. The Voravian army would be in a position to mount an attack the following day.

King Charles summoned Prince Rupert, the Duke of Flanders and Sir Walter Martley and, taking Peter as a messenger, set off to reconnoitre the battlefield. The five of them cantered ahead of the army until they arrived at the top of a small hill. The land dropped away before them, then rose steeply to a long crest. The tents and pennants of the Sloronians were clearly visible. The Voravian party reined in their horses.

'King François has certainly chosen a formidable position,' King Charles remarked. 'An assault up that hill will exhaust both our men and our horses.'

'I favour an immediate frontal attack,' was the duke's response. 'Do you remember the first battle you and I fought, sire? We simply rode pell-mell at the enemy and the rest of the army followed our example. It will be the same this time. The great love all our men have for you, our sovereign, will inspire them.'

Peter felt his heart lift. His reputation was already restored by report, but now, now he would be able to show everyone how he could fight.

'Flanders, of course I recall that battle. Often, when I'm feeling a bit out of sorts, I cheer myself up with its memory. But my old friend, you and I were in our twenties, not much older than my squire here. We were indestructible. Neither of us had responsibilities. Both of us were second sons. Now we are saddled with the cares and responsibilities of middle age. You have many dependants and I have a nation to care for. No, don't interrupt me. We've fought together, played, hunted, drunk and yes, wenched together. We are as brothers. There is no one I would rather have at my side in a hot scrap, but we must at least consider the alternatives to a frontal assault.'

'I am not sure we need attack.' Prince Rupert observed, 'François has withdrawn. He has acknowledged the power of our arms. I think it would be prudent to open negotiations with him.'

'Negotiate!' The duke exploded. 'François is still on our soil. He is taunting us. As I recall, it was you, Prince, who conducted the negotiations that led to the last peace. Part of the agreement was that we should scale down our garrisons at the castles at Forforn and Gwestern. Now what's happened? They've been overrun. I will never trust the word of the King of Sloronia. I may be just a simple soldier but I know a crafty dog when I see one.'

'Simple is a most apt description of your thinking, Flanders. You belong to a past age. One in which brawn was more valued than brain.'

'If this new age requires a man to renounce all the values of knightly conduct I want nothing to do with it. Though, I am sure, you will fit most comfortably there.'

The duke was purple with rage. Any moment now they would be demanding satisfaction by way of a duel.

'You'll be sorry for that insult one day. You forget that I'm the king's brother. I'm entitled to the respect due to royalty,' the furious prince snapped.

'I had not forgotten that you and King Charles share the same mother but that does not, I believe, make you part of the succession. However, I apologise for my hot words, they were spoken too hastily.'

'This must stop!' roared the king. 'I'll remind both of you that your enemy lies over there, not mounted on the horse next to you. The duke has offered an apology. I hope, Prince, you will accept it. I am against negotiating. We will do so from a position of weakness. Furthermore we have many freelances with us. They are expecting more than a daily rate. They anticipate some booty. Sir Walter, have you any suggestions?'

'I believe there is a chance we can outsmart King François, sire. May I explain my plan?'

Peter looked with admiration at the old warrior. His calm countryman's courtesy had for the moment deflected the ugly row.

'My good Sir Walter, you may indeed. If any man can find a way around this fix, it will be you.'

'I knows this part of the country. I was here but six months ago. It was on some minor business of yours, sire, a dispute between two local landowners.'

'Yes, I remember the occasion. You handled it with your usual skill and good sense. Go on.'

'The ridge we are looking at falls away steeply to the right, our right that is, and the Sloronians will, I be sure, have part of their force facing that direction. If you look over yonder to the left the land rises and the slope becomes like, as you might say, a precipice, so it does. The enemy will consider it not possible there can be a threat from there.'

Sir Walter turned his horse so that he was looking far to the left. The others followed the gaze of his single sighted eye.

'The face of yon cliff looks almost sheer from here,' Sir Walter explained, 'but you'll find there are two ways up it. One is steep and narrow, with many loose stones and some awkward rocks but the second one is not so steep and it's wider and even has some grassy parts. Its problem is that when you get to the top there's a very narrow gap, what you might call a defile, barely wide enough for two horses abreast.'

King Charles leant forward in his saddle, peering in the direction Sir Walter indicated. Peter and his fellow squires had had many lessons in tactics from Sir Walter, but those had been in the classroom or on the roof of the Harslanger. Now he was seeing the soldier's thinking in the context of a real battle. He listened intently to the plan as Sir Walter explained it in his homely brogue.

'If we can but get a body of mounted men up the second of those tracks, undetected, we will have outflanked the enemy. We will be above him and we will, moreover, have the advantage of surprise. We must see the enemy suspects nothing, so we must give him the idea that all our army are mustered here.'

'And how are we to achieve that?' The prince had accepted that the king was already persuaded of the scheme.

'We will only need mounted men. Certainly we will take the freelances, so the archers and pikemen can be drawn up as if ready to launch an attack. Then we should make a great show of parading the pennants of all our knights. Let them be borne about to the rear of the foot soldiers and by foot soldiers. With good luck the enemy will be watching our preparations and not detect the removal of our attacking force.'

'Sir Walter, you are a genius. You will, of course, command the attack. The duke and I will follow. Prince Rupert, you will organise the deception. We will take three squires as messengers.' The king was in high spirits.

'I would like to suggest my son, Henry, comes, but I fear his poor eyesight may prove an 'indrance. I confess 'tis a cause of some disappointment that Henry seems not to have a very warlike spirit. I believe he has inherited his peaceable nature from his dear mother.'

'Sir Walter, your Henry will, I am convinced, be a great man one day. When you and I are but a postscript to history, men will still be reading your son's poetry. My squire, Peter here, a friend of Henry's, recently passed me a book of his poems. I wept at many. Well, you will say, that's typical of an old soldier like me, but really his sonnet "To my grey-eyed lady" is one of the most beautiful I have read. I am, as you know, not much of a poet, more a musical man, but I would rather write half as well as young Henry Martley than win a few battles.'

'I never thought to hear you say that,' exclaimed the duke. 'If young Henry's poems become as popular as that air you composed, he will indeed go down in history. Incidentally I have often heard the men singing it as they marched. Who knows, it too may be around in a thousand years' time.'

'Oh, you mean my "Greensleeves"! I doubt it! That romantic King Henry in England is already claiming it. He is putting it about he wrote it for his new Queen.' The king laughed. 'Well, let us return to the army, I am full of optimism.'

Chapter 13

A STABLE-YARD FIGHTER

As they rode back Peter was beside Sir Walter.

The general turned to him and said, 'Well, Peter Salt, I must thank you. I would have done so at breakfast but did not wish to embarrass my son. Henry tells me that since your arrival at the palace, things have gone much better for him. It appears that you have put an end to much of the bullying he, as a short-sighted lad, has had to endure.'

'Henry and I have become very good friends,' Peter replied

'Well, all the same, I thank you for being kind.'

They rode on a short way then Sir Walter said, 'I understand you're worried that you returned to the duke to report on the bridge rather than throw your life away in a senseless fight. Indeed, you've had a nasty scrape as a result of your decision, so you have.'

'Yes, sir.'

'Well, my lad, learn two things from an old soldier like me. First, carry out your orders. If that means fighting a hopeless fight, well so be it, but if it means losing face with some colleagues or some sweetheart, don't worry. Second, wars always take longer than anyone expects. They are won with caution as much as with valour. Mind you, them that are sitting comfortably at home with their feet before the fire and their goblet to hand will not have it so.'

'So I was not a coward?'

'Only you can answer that, lad. But you obeyed the duke's orders. I would have done the same. And, for what it is worth, your action on guard duty and the way you have stood by your friend, my son, proves you have more than your fair share of guts.'

Peter bit his lip. It seemed the last of his worries had been removed.

After a pause, Peter said, 'The king seems convinced your plan will work.'

'I fear he doesn't appreciate the problem of the narrowness of the cleft we must pass through. I reckon it will take the best part of five hours to get three hundred mounted men through it and the noise is bound to alert the enemy.'

Peter was silent for a few minutes.

Then he asked, 'Could we not move up one day and attack the following one? The noise is a different matter.'

Sir Walter nodded. 'Aye, I believe we could move on the morrow and attack the next day. If we sent the men up in small parties at intervals we could be ready by dawn. The problem is the noise. Horse hooves on rock are confoundedly loud.'

'You said part of the path was grass, sir. How much?'

'Well, I really can't say.' Sir Walter scratched the back of his neck reflectively, 'When I came down it I were not paying particular attention. Perhaps a half, maybe more. The more I thinks about this attack, the more I feels we need to know more about that pathway. There be an old military saying that is somewhat overused but has much truth in it - time spent in reconnaissance is never wasted.'

Sir Walter caught up with the king and Peter saw the two men in deep discussion. Peter saw the king signal his agreement and Sir Walter turned, reined in his horse and waited until Peter drew level.

'His Majesty has suggested we take a close look now. I've arranged for my Henry to act as his squire whilst we're away. He said he'd be delighted to have the opportunity to be served by a civilized poet in place of a stable-yard fighter.'

Peter looked horrified, and was about to protest that he had hardly an aggressive drop of blood in his veins, when he noticed the twinkle in the old soldier's eye.

'Well, off we go. We've about two hours before darkness.'

Sir Walter turned his horse downhill following a faint track through the wood. Peter followed. They dropped down the hill and at length emerged at the foot of the valley. Ahead the slope was very steep. In places there were screes of stones. A brook ran along the valley and Sir Walter turned upstream, heading away from the enemy position from which they were hidden.

'We are in what soldiers call dead ground. It means that, due to the way the land rises and falls, we can't be seen,' Sir Walter explained.

Peter trotted along the track and Sir Walter pointed out the first way up. A little stream cascaded down through rocks. A narrow path skirted it.

'Too steep and rocky for us. The second track's a bit further on. I estimate we're about a mile upstream of the enemy's position.'

They were almost at the head of the valley, which was by now narrow with high slopes on both sides, when they came to the spot Sir Walter was heading for. Belle splashed through the brook and they began to ascend a small steep valley with another stream in it. Peter could see they were following a goatherd's path that climbed steadily up one side of the gully. Soon he was well above the stream that bubbled and gurgled below them. The track was so narrow they could not ride abreast. Its surface was grassy or sandy so their progress was reasonably silent.

As they climbed higher Peter became aware of a smell. At first it was barely a sensation but gradually it grew more powerful. By the time the track was some fifty feet above the torrent it was overpowering and foul. He was riding behind Sir Walter who had turned in his saddle to grimace at Peter. They rounded a corner and saw the cause. A sheep must have fallen from the cliff above them and had caught in a thorn bush that overhung the track. Its neck had wedged into a fork in the bush and after several hours of struggle it had died. Now, in the heat of the day, its decomposing corpse was rotting away.

Sir Walter stopped. 'We can't put our men through this.'

He was about to dismount when Peter forestalled him. He jumped down and drew his sword and approached the disgusting sight. Crows and vermin had reduced the head to a skull with a few wisps of black flesh and bits of wool. The body hung over the track, the belly purple and bloated.

Peter climbed up the side of the steep slope, steadied himself and hacked with his sword at the gnarled trunk of the thorn. The wood was old and hard; the blow from his sword jarred his wrist and made no impression on the bush. A second blow was no better and he almost lost his footing on the steep slippery grass. There was no choice; he would have to sever the neck. He wedged his feet into the turf and struck. The Toledo steel sliced through the tattered wool, the hardened skin and the vertebrae. A second blow and the body fell to the track, the belly rupturing. A flow of revolting liquid gushed out.

The smell was sickening. Peter prodded the skull with his sword and dislodged it from the bush. It rolled down onto the track. He climbed back down and kicked it over the edge. Now he had to deal with the body. He stood on the far side to the entrails and placed his hands inside the fleece. With a gasp he jumped back in horror. The putrid flesh was writhing with maggots. Gritting his teeth he pushed his hands back into the wool and seized the decomposing body. Trying to disregard the sensation of the squirming insects and the tearing of the brittle skin he dragged the decapitated sheep to the edge of the path and, for once overcoming his fear of heights, heaved it over. It slithered and somersaulted down into the ravine. The dreadful smell lifted. With the side of his foot he scooped the intestines over the side of the ledge.

'Well done, lad. Can't say I relished 'aving to do that.'

Peter sheathed his sword. He was shaking from disgust. For a few moments he stood with his forehead resting against Belle's warm wholesome flank breathing in her healthy scent. Then he remounted.

After about twenty minutes of climbing, the track swung round the shoulder of a hill and he could see that it rejoined the stream above a waterfall. By now there was a steep drop to their right and Peter, whose vertigo had now reasserted itself, clutched Belle's reins and prayed she did not suffer as he did.

The grass gave way to rock as they neared the head of the waterfall and then they could see the defile of which Sir Walter had spoken.

Sir Walter reined in and dismounted.

'Hold the horses. I'm going on foot from here.'

Peter dismounted and watched as Sir Walter walked cautiously into the gorge. He disappeared from view and Peter could hear nothing above the sound of the waterfall.

Ten minutes later Sir Walter reappeared.

'It's not as far through as I thought. You come out into a shallow valley. Perfect for assembling our force. Now let's return. I've been thinking about the practical problems of getting three hundred men up here on horseback, in single file, and quietly.'

They turned their horses and began to retrace their steps. The light was starting to fail and the downhill return with its steep drop was terrifying. By the time they reached the valley floor it was twilight. Sir Walter dug his heels in and the two cantered back downstream until they came to a clear path. They were back at the Voravian camp as night fell.

Campfires had been lit and some of the men had begun to sing. Mixed in with popular hymns and bawdy marching songs, Peter recognised the haunting melody of King Charles' 'Greensleeves' - its lyrics telling of love and contentment. That curious mixture of callousness and sentimentality, so characteristic of men at war, was asserting itself. The night was warmer than previous ones and there was a feeling that rain was coming.

Peter went to find the other squires. They were curious as to where he had been but, since Sir Walter had sworn him to secrecy, he could tell them nothing.

The following day the weather had broken and there was a steady drizzle. The king called a council of war attended by his generals.

'We attack on the morrow, very early. Sir Walter has devised a most sensible solution to the problem caused by King François' strong position. Sir Walter, would you be so good as to outline your plan?'

Peter watched as Sir Walter stepped forward.

'As His Majesty says, King François has what he must feel to be an impregnable position.'

Sir Walter went on to explain his plan. When he had finished there were a number of questions that he answered confidently.

The king summed up the meeting. 'I think we can be assured that Sir Walter has planned for every eventuality. It only remains to carry out his plan.'

Each general called together his captains and lieutenants and explained the part each was to play. Then the king summoned the entire army.

Peter, after being so much a part of the plan, surveyed the scene almost as if it were his army. It was a very mixed sight, ranging from magnificently arrayed noblemen, none more grandly attired than the Prince of Heinz-Coburg mounted on his sleek black stallion, to pikemen who stood in their sodden capes and looked as if they had just finished a hard day behind the plough. The freelances of the Company of the Fang formed a separate group.

In spite of Sergeant Watts' opinion and the encounter with Knud, there was an exciting aura about these men who lived by the sword. Some of the officers must be highly successful in their trade, for they were well mounted and in good physical condition. On his helm their commander, the *condottiere* the Count di Montelucca wore his famous yellow plumes.

The king explained what was required and that every man must carry out his part in the plan. He ended by saying generously that the plan was Sir Walter's and a cheer ran through the ranks. Peter had learnt that though there was much affection for King Charles there was an even greater faith in the ability of Sir Walter to win.

Sir Walter ordered a contingent of pikemen to collect a thousand bed mats. Then a small mounted party of knights under the High Constable - Sir Hugh Montague - Richard's father, were guided by Peter down to the valley floor and upstream to the beginning of the track. They tethered their horses and set off on foot. It took almost an hour to reach the defile for it was a hard ascent and silence was vital. When they reached the shallow valley of which Sir Walter had told Peter, they fanned out to watch for any enemy soldiers who might approach. Peter then returned by way of the familiar goat track. He remounted to return to the camp. As he cantered along he met a line of packhorses with the bed mats strapped to them. They were accompanied by a large party of pikemen under the command of some dozen captains.

When Peter reached the camp he could see that about half the knights and all the freelances had been divided into thirty squadrons, each with three or four packhorses to carry their armour and marshalled by Sir Walter's squire who had a sand timer on a small folding table. At half-hourly intervals a squadron would be despatched. The duke accompanied the leading squadron. The foot soldiers, together with the knights from the later squadrons, were busying themselves in making very obvious preparations for a frontal assault in full view of the Sloronians.

By the time the rain ceased and a mist began to hang over the sodden turf it was almost evening. It was then that the final squadron, accompanied by the king, mounted on Stang, and Peter left the camp. They left behind them the king's standard to mislead the foe into thinking King Charles was still in his camp.

The track down had by now been churned to a muddy swamp and it was a relief to reach the much firmer one that ran up the main valley. When they arrived at the start of the way up, they found Sir Walter and quite a crowd of men and horses. The ascent was taking longer than expected as Sir Walter insisted that there be a clear gap between each horse.

In the autumnal twilight the king's party set off, with Sir Walter, who looked exhausted from a day's organising, bringing up the rear.

Peter soon became aware of the plan to avoid noise. Where the track was not grassed it had been covered by bed mats, over which they rode at walking pace. To the side of each mat a pikeman had been placed with the task of straightening it should it become dislodged. At intervals, sergeants were posted to ensure this vital part of the plan was adhered to. As Peter passed Sergeant Schmidt he received a smart salute. Doubtless the little braggart was congratulating himself for being part of the same team. He saluted back with a smile. They passed the scene of the dead sheep and continued the ascent. The riders took the task of ensuring silence so seriously that the only sound was the creak of leather and the occasional snort of a horse. With luck these sounds would be drowned by the noise from the waterfall.

As the last of the day faded and the moon gave a soft misty light, they reached the defile and passed through it. Behind them came the pikemen gathering up the filthy bed mats. The valley beyond was full of men and horses. It was here that a most uncomfortable night would be spent.

Chapter 14

LIKE A BOW THROUGH THE WAVES

It was impossible to sleep. Everything was wet. The quartermaster had brought far too little bread and most of it was sodden. It was a long dismal night. The horses, seeming to sense the morrow's battle, stirred restlessly.

The first hint of dawn found the attacking force tired, hungry and anxious to get the business over with. There was now a fever of activity as knights unpacked their armour and were helped into it by their valets and squires.

Peter's first task was to fix Stang's armour and then that of Belle. Only when the horses had been protected did the task of armouring their riders begin.

Although King Charles had his valet to assist him in putting on his armour, Peter was also required to help. The king wore an undershirt and drawers of linen. Over this he pulled on a woollen jerkin to protect his body from the steel armour. It took the best part of an hour to strap on the various segments of steel that comprised the full panoply. All around similar scenes were being enacted

A few mounting stools had been brought up and squires raced around with them. Once all the knights had been helped into their saddles, Peter and the other squires, most wearing chain mail or leather jacks, mounted their own horses.

The king advanced to the top of the ridge, raised

his sword and touched Stang with his spurs. The rest of the force followed.

Peter had expected a wild gallop but in fact they cantered down the slope towards the Sloronians who were just stirring from their tents. The surprise was total. The next moment they were driving into the flank of the Sloronian army.

A pikeman turned to face Peter who raised his sword only to see Knud, his mouth wide in exhilaration, slash the man down. Peter was swept along in the charge. The shouts and screams of the wounded rang in his ears. He was light-headed with the sense of power the surprise had given them. He felt as he had in the stable, the red mist of fighting masking his vision. He lost sight of the king in the turmoil. In front of him a knight was struggling to mount a terrified horse. Belle, unable to move to either side, crashed into the man who fell under the weight of his armour. As he passed, Peter brought his sword down and watched it slide off the man's helm. They ploughed on. To his left the freelances, in a frenzy of bloodletting, were into the foot soldiers, hacking and slashing at men who had barely had time to understand what was happening. Bodies were falling on all sides. Peter looked to his right, and saw Prince Rupert's force advancing up the slope to attack from the front.

'This way, Peter,' a voice called and Peter recognised the king.

They plunged to the left towards a line of tents and pavilions. Stang's huge body seeming to drive a wedge through the panic-stricken enemy like a ship's bow through the waves. As they neared the grandest pavilion they were met by the first show of resistance. A score of well-armed and well-mounted knights began to advance towards them. They lowered their lances and formed into a wedge. Then the Duke of Flanders was at Peter's side together with a squadron of Voravians. With a thunderous crunch the two forces met. A lance hit Peter hard in the shoulder. The blow was so unexpected and so hard he was knocked backwards clean out of the saddle.

He fell to the ground, landing on his injured forearm. The pain hit him like a second blow. He looked up. Horse hooves were everywhere as, now in close combat, men smashed at each other. Two or three other men had been unhorsed and Peter climbed dazedly to his feet. He looked around for his sword. The next moment he received a terrific blow to the head.

There was a strange noise. It sounded like laughter. Peter lay still. His head throbbed, his arm felt dreadful. He slowly opened his eyes. The Duke of Flanders, his face dripping with sweat, stood above him laughing. He was holding Belle by her bridle.

'Well, what did you think of your first taste of battle, young man?'

Peter sat up. 'I did not do well,' he said. 'Perhaps I'm not cut out for fighting.'

'Oh, I don't think we need jump to that conclusion just yet.' The duke laughed. 'We've all taken a few knocks in our time. The important thing is to learn from them. Anyway the day is ours. The enemy has fled in complete disarray. We've captured no less than eight earls, three dukes and a pair of marquises. Those Sloronians seem to have more titles than they can surely need. We should collect some first rate ransoms. The freelances will be pleased. As for the tavern keepers, they won't believe their luck. Here, take your mare. She seems none the worse for her first battle.'

'Where is King François?' Peter asked, as he rubbed Belle below her forelock.

'Halfway back to Trois by now with his tail between his legs. Come and have a late breakfast, courtesy of King François' kitchen.'

'Trois? Where is that, sir?'

'It's about three to four days march from here, the nearest city in Sloronia and one of their greatest centres for trade and banking. I don't doubt but that King Charles, having given François a good whipping, will be thinking of seizing that rich city. Sloronia may be a far larger nation than Voravia but, I reckon, the balance of power has tilted greatly in our direction.'

Peter followed the duke towards the Sloronian tents. Everywhere he looked there were laughing, cheery Voravian foot soldiers, the same men who had looked so dejected in the rain the previous day, and miserable Sloronians preparing to drift back home, dispirited and in many cases clutching injuries.

At the tents, the victors formed lines to collect their breakfast, the lieutenants ensuring that their men fed before they did. The Duke was given a cheer as he passed. He paused to shake hands and thank different soldiers for their efforts.

They reached King François' tent and went in. King Charles was seated, still in full armour, at a desk. He looked up.

'I am sorry, sire. I fell off.' Peter had seldom felt so pathetic in his life.

King Charles looked up and gave a great burst of laughter.

'Well, you seem to have survived the experience, for which I am truly pleased. Help me out of this steel. Then get yourself a bowl of porridge and well, I think you could do with a mug of King François' most excellent claret.'

Peter drank his mug of claret. He had not enough experience of clarets to know whether or not it was excellent. But one thought cheered him. It seemed no one regarded his performance in too bad a light. As he thought back over his first experience of action he heard a great cheer ahead of him. A huge throng of men were grouped around the king who had his right hand aloft grasping the left hand of Sir Walter, the true victor of that day.

'King François is no match for us, so long as we have Sir Walter,' the king shouted and the army responded with laughs and cheers. 'Those good souls who gave up their bed mats will find plenty of replacements to choose from. Well fought everyone!'

Peter waited until the king and Sir Walter had finished complimenting different soldiers and returned to the tent to complete the administrative tasks the end of fighting involved. He went in and heard the king asking the prince to report on the losses the Voravian army had incurred. They were remarkably light. The most senior was the Earl of Harford. His death had not been in battle. The earl had partaken of too much claret prior to joining the prince's advance up the hill. He had fallen from his horse and broken his neck

The prince then said, 'My squire took a serious blow to his leg. Your surgeon, the friar, reports that he will be unable to serve for a while. As Ferdinand le Gray seems a keen young man, I would like to have him serve me for at least the remainder of the campaign.'

The king could hardly object and Ferdinand was summoned to receive his new post. Peter watched the appointment. Ferdinand could barely conceal his delight in what could only be reckoned a promotion.

As the pair of them left the pavilion he turned a grinning face to Peter and said, 'Well, little apothecary, it seems we will be seeing more of each other. I have not forgotten either your behaviour to me in the stable or your cowardice on the Mintz. I am not a man to forgive.'

Chapter 15

THE SIEGE

The next morning, when Peter attended the monarch, the king explained that he would be busy all day with the long and complicated procedure for ransoming the various high-value captives. He would send them back to Nieuport under escort where they would be lodged in the prison block at the palace, the Dark Tower.

Peter watched the preparations for the departure. He was surprised to see that the Sloronian nobles would travel in considerable style. It was hardly necessary to guard them too strenuously as to escape would be against the code of chivalry. He listened to much light-hearted discussion, often involving the gentlemen themselves, as to who was worth the most.

Once the prisoners were off King Charles' hands he turned to the question of opening negotiations with the Sloronian crown.

'I could send the duke but I'm afraid he would most certainly lose his temper at the first sign of a bargaining offer,' the king confessed to Peter, 'so it will be the prince. He is much better endowed with the subtleties of diplomacy.'

The following morning the prince, accompanied by his new squire now proudly wearing the bejewelled medallion with the prince's motif of a hound, and twenty knights set off under a flag of truce to contact the Sloronians. Peter and Henry were glad to see the back of Ferdinand. It would be some days before he returned.

As the duke had forecast, King Charles chose to press home his military advantage and advance on Trois. The weather remained overcast with rain threatening but morale was high. The mounted men rode up and down the line to show solidarity with the ordinary soldiers who marched along singing and joking.

At midday they crossed the border into Sloronia and shortly the countryside changed. The ground rose and became sandy and barren. There was hardly any sign of farming, only a few sheep and goats, and the homesteads were miserably poor. The army's rations reflected the change in circumstances.

'This has to be the nastiest silverbrord I've ever tried to eat, Henry. We win a great victory and end up with this trash.' He waved a piece of skin and gristle at his friend.

'It is not really my lord's fault, although he will surely get the blame. When we were in Voravia, he allowed the quartermaster a generous allowance to pay for provisions. The idea being that, once we were in Sloronia, we would live off the land by seizing food and fodder as we advanced. But you only have to look at this,' Henry indicated the desolate heathland, 'there's just nothing to seize.'

That evening the latest foraging party returned with a pitiful amount. Peter overheard Flanders berating the unfortunate quartermaster and purser.

'You should have bought more when you could. Soldiers do not appreciate hunger. Morale will suffer.'

'We must press on as fast as we can,' King Charles intervened. 'When we take Trois we will have plenty to fill our bellies.'

It took four days of hard going before the ground fell away and, lying at the mouth of a wide river, they saw the great walled city of Trois. Peter had not expected it to be so large or so well fortified. Although not the capital city of Sloronia it seemed larger than Nieuport.

As Peter, following the king, approached the walls the prince met them. He had serious news to impart.

'King François is mortally ill. He took an injury at the battle and it has become infected. It is thought he will shortly die. It was impossible for me to see him, of course, but the Bishop of Trois had been appointed as his representative. The bishop, a man a damn sight more suited to the battlefield than the cloister, resolutely refused to negotiate. I remained at the Sloronian royal household in Villa Real for three days but it was apparent there would be no change in the bishop's attitude.'

The Duke of Flanders, on the king's right, was about to explode, when the king raised a conciliatory hand.

'We must think before we react. I accept, Prince, that you've done your best. You are a fine diplomat.' At this the duke snorted and muttered something impolite. The king continued, 'I've two questions.

Who will command the Sloronian army and where is the Prince of Sauterns, the heir to the throne?'

'The army is under the command of the Duke D'Urbin, King François' second son. He's a hot-headed, ambitious man. As for the Prince of Sauterns, he is still at the capital. He is, as you know, a deeply religious man. Not unsurprisingly the Bishop of Trois appears to have nothing but contempt for the probable new king with his piety.'

King Charles thanked the prince again for his efforts.

He turned to his Treasurer, the Earl of Bardsey. 'How are our finances? I am worried that once the freelances hear about the problem with the ransom, we'll have trouble with them. It may be advisable to pay them off here and now.'

The earl, a stout gentleman with receding hair, removed his spectacles from his nose, wiped his eyes on his lace cuff and replied in his formal way.

'I have been as prudent as possible, sire, but it would be misleading to pretend that I was not relying on receiving substantial ransom sums. We could discharge the mercenaries but, if we do, we will be very low in gold.'

The duke had been impatiently shifting his weight from one foot to the other and now seized the chance to say, 'We must take the city. Then all our problems are solved. We'll restore our exchequer. We'll give the bishop something to make him yield, and whoever sits on the throne of Sloronia, he will have to negotiate.'

'I agree with you, Duke,' said the king, 'but it will

be no easy task. We'll surround the city and we must bar the waterway in. In the meantime we'll assemble the siege engines. This could be a lengthy campaign. I will speak with di Montelucca, and with luck, he'll persuade them to chance the prospects of a successful siege.'

The following day Peter watched as half the Voravian army, under the prince, crossed the river two miles upstream with the object of completing the surrounding of the city. Peter and Henry would, at least, be spared Ferdinand's taunts.

A week later news reached the Voravians that King François had died.

And so for three months the two armies and the citizens of Trois endured ever more desperate conditions. The siege engines proved useless. They were neither tall enough nor stable enough to allow the archers to fire over the walls. Quickly abandoned they stood, mired in mud, like reproachful spectres looming over the Voravian army.

After the first month, Peter learned that the commandant of the freelances had come to King Charles and told him that his men wished to be paid off. The Earl of Bardsey had apparently managed to do this.

''T'wouldn't surprise me if that rapacious di Montelucca, having exhausted our treasury, doesn't go straight to the Sloronians to offer them his services,' King Charles muttered.

Food soon ran out, as did fodder. Most of the draught oxen and some of the packhorses were slaughtered but there was almost no firewood and the meat had to be eaten uncooked. It was almost inedible. The acute shortage of fit men meant that new latrines were not dug so that the existing ones were overflowing. Clothes and bodies went unwashed in the surrounding filth.

By the end of the second month, in appalling weather, plague broke out in the city and soon spread to the besieging Voravians.

Fear now gripped the army. It was the randomness of the infection that was its most awful characteristic. Some days there would be a hope that it had passed, only for a surge of cases. The spectre of death stalked the ranks. It struck at all. Highborn and serf - no one was safe. Among the squalor, Peter came across Sergeant Schmidt who lay dying in a stinking hovel. The sergeant gave Peter a wan smile and extended a hand that was both freezing and damp. Peter took it and managed to thank his one-time tormentor for his support. Schmidt's corpse was dumped, along with twenty-four more, in a hastily dug pit that evening. The busiest men were the priests and the gravediggers. Like everyone, Peter's body became infested with lice and fleas. There were rats everywhere. But even more disgusting were the huge, pale, fat worms that gorged on the dead. They, and the fear of plague, haunted Peter's nightmares. The sodden, fetid air stank of despair.

Each morning Peter examined his own body fearfully for the tell-tale rash and the boils under the armpits. Like everyone, he prayed desperately to be spared.

Then a fleet of Sloronian ships broke the blockade on the river. The news spread to the besiegers that the city was replenished and that the new King François III had formed an army and placed it under the command of his brother, the Duke D'Urbin. As King Charles had anticipated, the Count di Montelucca's Company of the Fang were now on the Sloronian payroll.

King Charles called a council.

'I shall lift the siege tomorrow. If we remain here there is every likelihood we will be pressed to fight in this impossible position. Our ranks are so much depleted, I'm sure no one believes we will now be able to force the city to surrender. D'Urbin is almost certain to pursue us once he sees we have withdrawn. We are not safe yet, but with luck, we will at least be able to choose our battle-ground.'

Even the Duke of Flanders had to agree. The king put his decision in writing, sealed it with his Great Seal and the squires delivered it to the generals commanding the forces around the city walls.

The next day the siege was lifted and the Voravian army began its retreat. Peter, like the rest of the army, greeted the news of the withdrawal with a sense of relief. Surely things would get better as they neared their homes.

As the army wound its way up the hill and away from Trois, he looked back at the site of the disaster. A scene of desolation lay below him. The mud was studded with carts from the baggage train, pathetic shelters and the mounds and pits in which the dead had been buried. Above them towered the useless siege-engines like so many gravestones. The sickly-sweet reek of death, disease and excreta drifted up on the wind towards him. A slow insistent rain began to fall.

The awfulness of the place reinforced his new view of war. No longer was it an opportunity for adventure. It was cold, filthy, degrading and too often led to a pitiful end.

Chapter 16

THE RETREAT

He was going to die. Although they appeared to have escaped the plague, fever raged throughout the army. Exhausted, emaciated and shivering in his stinking, sodden rags his will to live had drifted away. Behind them the pursuing Sloronian force would be urged on by the detritus of the retreat, the discarded equipment, the dead and partly consumed animals, the abandoned wounded and the pitiful little burial mounds. By the morrow a hopelessly one-sided battle would be joined and what remained of the Voravian army would be cut down on this desolate wasteland.

The weather was sometimes wet and windless; sometimes the rain held off but a cold wind blew out of the north; sometimes it was both wet and windy. Belle plodded wearily along. Peter longed for the warmth of his mother's kitchen.

He thought of Lucy and, for the hundredth time, cursed the moment he had told her that he had fought for Elspeth. A wave of misery flooded over him. He dropped his reins, cupped his hands to his mouth and blew into them then rubbed them vigorously together in an attempt to get them warm. He looked back to check on the two horses on leading reins tethered to his saddle, the great black warhorse, Stang and the king's much lighter riding horse, Zephyr. The king, himself, was on foot striding along the slow-moving column, encouraging his men as much by his example as by his words. His army's most valued possession, its morale, was shattered.

In the presence of their monarch, spirits would be lifted but soon the cold, hunger and presence of death reasserted their grip on the force. At the head of the column rode Prince Rupert, Sir Walter and a squadron of knights attended by their squires. Next in the column came the hungry, weary foot soldiers, their clothes reduced to shreds. Some had lost their boots and their feet were wrapped in bloodstained rags, others were barefoot, they carried their pikes and bows listlessly. Before the war they had been ploughmen or herders of stock and now all they could think of was returning to their peacetime work. They trudged along through the mud, their heads down, their shoulders hunched against the bitter wind.

Behind the walking men came the heavy wooden carts of the baggage train, the oxen seemingly to take one step every minute. The carts were continually getting bogged down in the mud and ruts. A few of the sick and wounded had been placed in the carts but each evening of the retreat those who had breathed their last were unceremoniously removed, one of the priests said a short prayer and the body was hastily buried. The rest of the baggage consisted of the small amount of provisions left and the armour and a few tents for the knights.

At the rear the king had placed the remainder of the knights under the duke. Every morning the duke would send a small contingent of mounted men back to bring reports of the pursuing Sloronian army. In much better shape, not having had to endure the hardships of the siege, and not encumbered by oxen, it was closing fast. It was now but half a day's march behind the fleeing Voravians.

The route they were taking was the shortest one back, but it still entailed the high barren plateau they had crossed three months earlier. If it had been bad then, it was infinitely worse now in midwinter. They had passed through a small hamlet, little more than a few dejected huts with sodden thatch, the previous day and failed to find any food or fodder for the animals. Since then they had hardly seen a sign of human activity. Occasionally a few thin trees broke the monotony of the high plain.

A sad stench of unwashed men, sickness and defeat hung over the retreat. Above circled the carrion-eating black kites on outstretched wings watching the slow line of men creep across the plain like one of the diseased and loathsome worms.

Peter found in Henry the only source of comfort. Just as he had shrugged off the bullying in the Harslanger, the poet appeared to be able to see through the immediate misery of the turn of events since the victory.

'Well, they do say in the foulest midden there's a lost florin hidden although I confess, it takes some finding.' He paused, then added, 'I'm searching and do you know, I think I've found it. I believe the supply of silverbrord has finally run out. As an alternative, starvation seems quite attractive.'

Peter managed a laugh. 'I wouldn't count on it.

These last months have taught me that just when you think things can get no worse they do.'

'Ah, so your spies have unearthed a cartload of sausages.'

Peter saw little of le Gray. When they met the man seemed less aggressive. Their concentration on survival had pushed their animosity into the background. He remarked on the improvement to Henry.

'I suppose I should say that this is yet a further example of that elusive florin but I'm not entirely convinced.'

'Why is that?'

'He's probably decided you are a match for him. He's withdrawn from that battle to concentrate on his real foe, me.'

'Well, Henry, you know you have an ally in me.'

'Ah, but I'm not sure I wouldn't prefer Ferdinand as my enemy than you as my ally. At least he doesn't offer to share his silverbrord with me. Incidentally, have you heard? Ferdinand is something of a hero.'

'Go on.'

'Well, apparently during the course of blockading the river approach at Trois, three soldiers fell into the water when their boat capsized. Of course, none of them could swim. But Ferdinand plunged in and succeeded in saving two of them. It turns out that, in addition to being a complete swine he swims like a fish. Curious mixture that - pig and fish. I'm surprised somebody responsible for feeding this army hasn't combined the two into some disgusting sausage.

Although, come to think of it, that would explain last night's issue.'

Peter noticed a small change in the weather; the wind seemed to be dropping. It was definitely less cold and the sky had darkened, with a hint of purple and yellow, like a bruise. A few large snowflakes began to fall.

Roger de Vers, one of the squires, cantered back from the head of the column and asked Peter where the king was.

'He's back towards the carts,' Peter replied.

'I've a message from Sir Walter,' Roger said.

'Take Zephyr,' said Peter, unhitching the lighter horse and passing the leading rein to Roger.

A minute or two later the king, now mounted, and the duke were back. Peter joined them as they hurried up the line.

When they reached the front Sir Walter and Prince Rupert met them. The van of the army had paused at the crest of a gentle slope that fell away before them to a brook with steep sides. It was quite possibly the lower reaches of the stream they had followed on their way to the great victory three months earlier.

The track led down the slope and crossed the brook on a narrow stone bridge with parapets on either side. The land then rose to the edge of a forest and he could discern, through the gathering murk of the evening and the snow, that there was a distinct alteration in the landscape. It was more hilly, more wooded, and almost certainly more fertile.

'I fear the baggage carts will not pass the bridge,'

the prince remarked.

'Well, we'll knock the sidewalls off it,' the Duke of Flanders snapped.

The king turned to his generals. 'Let us be frank. Sooner or later we're going to have to fight. The army think that now we've crossed the frontier we will be safe. But the Duke D'Urbin won't stop for a line on the map. He will press on his advantage. Every hour of this retreat increases his chances and reduces ours. Better to stand and fight, whilst we still have some energy, than be forced ever further back. We'll pitch our camp at the edge of the trees. We can make fires. The men can get warm and their spirits will rise. Even this weather may help us. I've never fought in a snowstorm and I'm damn sure neither has D'Urbin. His advantage in the numbers and freshness of his men will be blunted. Prince Rupert, take a party of men to break down those stonewalls and then arrange matters for the camp. As soon as possible get some fires going. Once the army sees them it will give them good heart. Flanders and Sir Walter, come with me. I want to look at the field of battle with D'Urbin's eyes. Rupert, your squire can take Stang with him to the camp.'

A small party comprising the king, the Duke of Flanders, Sir Walter and their three squires made their way slowly along the crest. The ground around them was rapidly turning white as the snow continued to fall. Only the black line of the brook broke the soft white blanket.

As Peter looked, something stirred in his mind.

He struggled to place it. He was sure he could see the scene. He was in his father's shop with Lucy and it was their very first lesson. What was it Lucy had said? No. No it wasn't Lucy it was something his father had mentioned when they were investigating the properties of water. Then he remembered what it was.

He rode up to the old general.

'Sir Walter,' he began.

'Aye, lad, don't be afraid. I've been in worse straits in my time. We'll pull through. Though, I dare wager, there'll be much blood lost the morrow.'

'No, it's not that, Sir Walter, I've got an idea.'

Peter had pulled up and was looking down the slope.

Sir Walter reined in his horse.

'Now that's more like it. I know you've got a brain in that young head o'yorn. Well, spit it out, ideas are no use if you keep 'em to yourself. And don't worry if it don't come out quite like you'd like it to. I set more store by a good idea said simple and true, than any amount of high-flown rhetoric.'

Peter took a deep breath.

'Suppose, sir, you were the Duke D'Urbin and you arrived here and looked across at our army on the far hill, you would be thinking how do we cross that brook, wouldn't you?'

'He would. And he would quickly call up his engineers, so he would, to throw bridges across. He'll have planks and beams with his baggage-train, you can depend upon it. It'll delay him. But he's in no hurry.'

‘Yes, but Sir Walter,’ and Peter, hesitantly at first, but with growing confidence as Sir Walter showed his interest, began to explain his idea.

When he had finished Sir Walter turned to him and his tough old face was split by a broad grin. He pulled the gauntlet from his right hand and leant down from his warhorse.

‘Give me your hand, young man. Let me be the first to shake the hand of a future general. There‘s not a moment to lose. I’ll go speak to the king.’

Sir Walter spurred his horse and Peter saw him speak earnestly to the monarch. King Charles reined in Zephyr, turned her around and cantered back.

‘Well done, Peter. From what Sir Walter tells me you have just changed the odds on tomorrow’s battle. Now I want you to stay here with me. Sir Walter and the duke will arrange everything. With the parapet to the bridge removed that should not alert D’Urbin. I reckon we have two to three hours to complete the subterfuge. There must be no tracks left in the snow to alert the foe.’

The king rode slowly along the ridge, scrutinising the battlefield from the enemy’s likely position. He was assessing the extent of the enemy’s view.

‘Once everyone’s crossed the bridge we’ll smooth the ruts the carts will make. We don’t want the enemy to see which way the track goes.’

The king turned to Peter. He had a faraway look in his eyes.

‘A hundred years ago, on St. Crispin’s day, my ancestor, King Henry the fifth of England, won a famous victory against fearful odds. With God's blessing tomorrow will see as great a triumph.'

'What victory was that, sir?" Peter asked

'Why Agincourt, of course. It's sad but England hasn't produced a king in a hundred years to compare with Harry. I reckon that nation's as good as doomed.'

They began to make their way back along the ridge as the last wagon crossed the bridge and began its slow ascent of the slope. Fires were already blazing and they could see the duke urging the captains and footmen to cut saplings and boughs from the forest.

'Let us see how much progress has been made. We've got two hours at most.'

Chapter 17

'GOD SAVE KING CHARLES'

The king led the way across the bridge and turned downstream to watch the work.

It was apparent that Sir Walter, with his talent for organisation, had given much thought as to the best way to put Peter's idea into practice within the short time available. He had divided the brook into sections of about twenty chains. Fifty men were responsible for each length, with an extra fifty allocated to the three divisions furthest from the woodland; it would take longer to drag the branches there. In each group of fifty, half were employed in hacking down the saplings and branches, five sharpened some of the stouter poles for what Sir Walter termed his nasty surprise, fifteen used the packhorses to drag the poles and branches down and five arranged the wood over the stream. A captain commanded each party. Knights and foot soldiers worked side by side.

Peter and the king watched as the sharpened staves were driven into the bed of the stream, then poles laid across from one bank to the other and finally a covering of branches and brushwood thrown on top. At occasional intervals a plank from the baggage train was in place across the brook.

Sir Walter met them. He was in the best of moods, fairly glowing with enthusiasm and energy.

'Those planks, Sir Walter, no doubt they are to serve some purpose. May I ask what it is?'

'Certainly, sire. When all is ready, we'll send a few men across them, up to the ridge. It's what D'Urbin would expect us to do. To keep a lookout for his approach. When he comes in sight they'll return across them planks. Their footprints in the snow should help persuade the Sloronian command it is safe to attack. And I've had a further thought. We need to encourage an attack tomorrow. The snow may melt if we wait.'

'Very true, Sir Walter. Now do not disappoint me. I know you have a plan to achieve that.'

'Once we've finished here we'll move most of the carts down the hill to the edge of the stream, so we will. D'Urbin will realise he has an opportunity to attack before we are ready.' Sir Walter went on to describe the second part of the scheme.

'Oh, capital, the more I hear of it the more I like it.'

The king leapt from his horse and began to throw branches onto the poles.

The men around him who, two hours ago had been trudging exhaustingly, gave a shout of 'God save King Charles,' and redoubled their effort.

Peter and the king began to make their way up the slope to the camp.

'Tell me, Peter, does your mother still cook a rabbit stew?'

'Yes, sir, indeed she does.'

'Well, when this wretched war is over, I shall invite myself to supper. It's one of the privileges of royalty. My mouth is already watering at the prospect.

How I remember that evening when we first met! It remains one of my happiest.'

The last of the short winter twilight finally faded as the task was completed. The carts were hauled down the slope to the edge of the brook and turned around so that they faced uphill. Hazel rods had been bent above them and sacks thrown over the top. The tired, but satisfied, soldiers trudged back up the hill to where the cooks had, on the Prince's instructions, used the last of the provisions for the evening meal. It was, nevertheless, a very meagre one.

That night there was but little sleep. Men huddled around the fires and the chaplains moved through the army, hearing confessions and writing short letters addressed to parents, wives and sweethearts. Peter wrote a brief note to his parents and entrusted it to Brother Simon, who blessed him. Then he set off through the encampment to find Henry. The snow fell around the army, spitting in the fires and coating everything in its gentle embrace. Men's faces, lit from below by the fires and framed against the night sky, took on the appearance of demons. Yet there was a strange, soft beauty to the scene. Friendships, forged over the long months of the campaign, were suddenly sharpened by the imminence of possible death. When people spoke it was more often than not in whispers as if they were in some enormous cathedral. It was easy to believe, as the priests told them, that they were under God's care.

Peter came across the young poet sitting on a log gazing into the flames. Peter eased him to one end of the log and sat down beside him.

He threw an arm round the thin shoulders and said cheerily, ‘Well, old friend, tomorrow will bring either death or glory. You poets like to deal in these big issues, so you should be in your element. Come what may, if one of us is to perish and one survive, let him who lives remember our friendship for ever.’

‘If we do get through, what will you do with the rest of your life, Peter?’

‘I’ve been thinking quite a lot about that,’ Peter replied. ‘Ever since I saw that Portuguese caravel I’ve been dreaming of sailing west to the New World. I wonder if King Charles would let me lead an expedition to found a colony in his name over there. And you, my man of letters, what of you?’

‘Well, as you know I’ve been writing at every opportunity. And not just poetry. I’ve taken to writing plays. There is a new interest in the theatre. Not just the old mystery plays, but dramas that deal with politics, history, love and real people. I’ve nearly finished a play that tells of a doomed love affair between a boy and girl from different classes. He’s a noble. She a milkmaid.’

‘Does it have a happy ending?’

‘No, no. Of course not. It’s a tragedy. Nearly everyone dies.’ Henry laughed.

‘Oh dear. Henry could you, perhaps, write something a little more jolly?’

‘Well, I do have an idea for a comedy. It’s about two identical twins. They get separated at birth and then find themselves in the same city, unbeknown to each other and…'

'And they both fall in love with the same girl?'

'Yes of course. But here's the twist. She has this very plain elder sister her father desperately wants to get married off, so she - the pretty one that is - sends a letter to her lover, telling him to visit at dead of night and she will run away with him.'

'Go on, Henry.'

'Of course both twins get the letter as does the sister. Both turn up and on this magical night it's not the pretty sister who is waiting and…' There was a long pause.

'And what?'

'Ah, you will have to come to the play.'

'It sounds wonderful. I shall delay my voyage to the New World until I have seen it.'

Henry turned to Peter. 'Peter Salt, we've been the best of friends. The wide world will judge us very different sorts of men. But I know that inside your tough exterior there's something quite gentle. At least I think there is. When you said you fought for Princess Lucia and the others laughed, I knew you would make a fine champion for any lady, however highborn.'

There was something about the wistful way Henry spoke that made Peter look quizzically at his friend. Henry was staring into the fire.

Then it dawned on Peter. Henry was in love with Lucy. He should have known ages ago. Of course, a romantic and a poet like Henry would be bound to be desperately in love. So Henry's 'grey-eyed lady' was none other than the princess. It was a bit inconvenient that they should both fancy the same girl, but now was not the time to fall out. Who knew what tomorrow would bring? Until then he would lift his friend's spirits.

'Oh, I've quite changed my allegiance. From now on, it's Elspeth.' Peter laughed. 'The princess knows. I told her.'

Henry turned his head slowly and a soft smile flitted across his lips. Peter gave a vigorous nod and shrugged.

'Well, I must say I'm not surprised you took Ferdinand's advice to heart. For come to think of it, Elspeth is an excellent choice. I congratulate you. I was thinking I might make a pitch for her myself. But, Peter, now I know she's your sweetheart, I'll hold off. Yes, honest, I will. Does she know? Have you written pledging your undying love or is she just a soldier's trifle?'

'Well, no, I haven't written. But I might. Do you think I should?'

'Oh undoubtedly. Girls set great store by that sort of thing. Even if she can't read, you could always send a note covered with kisses. Peter I had no idea you were smitten. But, don't worry. I'll tell not a soul.'

'What of you, Henry? Have you a girl back home?' Peter asked, fearful that his friend would reveal that he and Lucy were secretly betrothed. 'And do you write to her?'

Henry paused for a moment then said, 'Well yes I do, but I don't think she reciprocates my affection. I ply her with poems. Most girls like that sort of thing, but I'm not sure about mine. Sometimes I wish I were a warrior like you or Ferdinand. Now, my lovelorn swain, I think we both deserve a drink. The king has invited his generals to his tent and I'm sure the king's squire and the treasurer's squire are part of the party.'

It was evident Henry's was a secret love.

They made their way through the dream-like setting of the camp, moving from one blaze of light into inky blackness then back into another. All the while the veil of snow hid everything but the immediate surroundings.

They arrived at the royal tent. In the antechamber there was quite a press of attendants including Ferdinand le Gray, finely attired as Prince Rupert's squire and sporting, around his neck, the magnificent jewel Peter had first seen at the skirmish at the bridge over the Mintz.

The king and the duke strode out to check on the weather.

'Ah, what have we here? The poet and the soldier. With such talent, the kingdom will be safe for the next fifty years.'

'I suspect we may have more use for the soldier come the morrow,' the duke responded.

Ferdinand came across, holding a goblet of wine.

'Well Salt, appears I owe you an apology. I don't shuppose we shall ever be friends but perhaps we can reshpect each other.' He took a long draught from his goblet. 'I must give credit where it's due. I'm told we have you to thank for tomorrow's plan.

Sheems I underestimated you. Hope you'll accept my congratulations. Let's hope your plan works.' He belched. 'For, if we lose tomorrow, not only will most of us perish, there will be nothing between D'Urbin and Nieuport. Voravia will be annexed by Sloronia.' Ferdinand nodded extravagantly and extended his hand and the astonished Peter could do nothing other than shake it.

Ferdinand took another swig from his tankard.

'Didn't 'spect to shee you here Henry. Thought you'd be with your books.' He had evidently been drinking heavily.

Ferdinand swaggered off.

'Well, I never expected to hear that,' Henry remarked, 'but he's no fool and however little he has inherited from his illustrious ancestor, he is at least a patriot.'

'Oh, I never doubted that. In many ways I wish he weren't. It would be easier to hate him.' As Peter said this, a small part of him had to acknowledge his pleasure in Ferdinand's approval.

As the two of them returned to their tents they noticed a change in the weather. It was colder and fresher. It was still snowing, but the large wet flakes had changed to small, finer ones.

The full gravity of the morrow's action was, as Ferdinand had said, now clear. If it resulted in defeat, it would mean the end of his nation's independence. The stakes could not be higher. His plan had to work

Chapter 18

THE BATTLE IN THE SNOW

Dawn was a barely discernible lightening. The snow continued to fall, blanketing the land. Peter could hardly see twenty yards. Men floundered about trying to get warm. Branches were hacked down to feed the fires, but there was a feeling of thankfulness that the long night was past. The day would settle matters one way or another.

Peter's old instructor, Sergeant Ben Watts, with two other sergeants, sought him out.

'Well sir, I knew from the way you 'andled your sword from the word go, as 'ow you'd make a fine soldier one day. An' it turns out I were right. Well anyways, sir, me and me mates, we want to say how well you done to come up with the plan for today's battle. I've done me share of fighting under Sir Walter but he ain't getting no younger. T'would be a fine thing to have someone with his brains to take over when he hangs his sword up.'

Peter thanked him.

'If I can ever be of service to you, just ask for me.' Watts touched his cap and plodded off with his mates into the snow and down towards the carts.

Under cover of the snowstorm, Peter was aware that Sir Walter's plan was being put into effect. Knights buckled on their armour and made their way down the hill followed by archers and foot soldiers. Back in the camp all was bustle as the rest of the army made a show of preparing to withdraw.

'We must expect an attack from the flanks as well as a frontal assault,' King Charles had written in a message to Prince Rupert that Peter had carried. The prince was to hold back a squadron on the crest to deal with it.

By mid-morning the snow eased off and the clouds drifted away to reveal a beautiful winter's day. Peter could see that his idea had worked as perfectly as he could have hoped. The snow had behaved exactly as his father had described all those years ago.

There was not a breath of wind and the shouts of the men heaving on the carts or encouraging the horses hung in the crystal air.

Peter saw a small party of scouts running down the far side of the valley, presumably with news of the Sloronian advance. Without hesitating they crossed the brook on two of Sir Walter's planks and began the ascent towards the Voravian lines. As they did so a stupendous sight erupted on the crest of the far hill. It was the Sloronian army in full battle array.

Peter could imagine the sense of destiny that must have engulfed the Duke D'Urbin when he saw that his enemy was at his mercy, unprepared for an attack and preoccupied in trying to retrieve the baggage train.

There came a trumpet blast and the attack began. The Sloronian cavalry started its advance down the hill, the horses' hooves throwing up plumes of snow that twinkled and sparkled in the sunlight. Peter picked out the Duke D'Urbin. He was in a splendid dark blue suit of armour with a magnificent plume of red and gold feathers on his helmet. He was at the head of the centre squadrons. To his left and right he could see other squadrons led by the flower of Sloronian nobility, their pennants and plumes making a bold picture against the snow.

About twenty yards behind the leading squadrons further ones followed in a second wave. There must have been over a thousand mounted men but he could see no sign of di Montelucca's yellow plumes. Even without the mercenaries, had the two armies met on equal terms, the result would not have been in doubt.

Then, moments before the leading Sloronians, now at full gallop, reached the brook King Charles gave the order for a signal to be sounded. The archers ceased heaving on the wheels and seized their bows and arrows from where they had hidden them beneath the carts. The hessian was thrown off and the knights, who had been hidden in the carts, began to spill out. Peter watched as D'Urbin, sensing a trap, tried to rein in, but it was too late. The next moment the snow-laden branches that had hidden the brook gave way and horses and riders plunged headlong into the stream.

Some did manage to stop, but those behind crashed into them. The air was full of the screams of horses and men. Dismounted knights were trying to climb out but they were weighed down by their armour and unable to get any purchase on the slippery ground.

The horrified second wave of Sloronian cavalrymen attempted to wheel their warhorses as they saw their front rank disappear into the brook. But it was mostly impossible. The tilt of the icy ground meant that hooves could find no grip. Then the rank behind cannoned into them and forced many into the maelstrom of flailing hooves and struggling men. Those that succeeded in pulling up had to attempt to turn their mounts against the oncoming charge. Broadside on to the Voravian archers, now only twenty yards away, they presented an easy target. Volley after volley of steel-tipped arrows tore into the terrified horses, bringing the squealing beasts crashing down. The Voravian knights advanced on foot to the brook and beheld the struggling enemy knights as they tried to extricate themselves from the confusion. Wielding maces and axes they hacked at those who attempted to climb the bank on the Voravian side.

The carnage was appalling. Horses collapsed, throwing their riders into the snow, now turning crimson with blood. With their leadership floundering in the water, crushed by the weight of their armour or by the second wave of cavalry, complete confusion reigned. Now the Voravian knights began to pour across the planks and into the chaos of fallen men and horses, slashing at the terrified Sloronians with axes and maces.

King Charles had posted the duke in the copse close to the bridge and, once the trap had been sprung, he had led his men out and along the far bank to cut off any retreat. This party now arrived behind the retreating and demoralised Sloronians and hurled themselves into the throng to complete the rout.

King Charles turned to his bugler.

‘Sound the signal to call off the fighting. We’ll end the slaughter before all the prizes are killed.’

Within less than thirty minutes a proud army had been utterly destroyed. Peter, who in the earlier battle had felt exhilarated by the excitement of his participation, now, as a spectator, felt sickened at the massacre.

The king, accompanied by the Earl of Bardsey and Peter, rode down to the brook. Knights, pikemen and archers stood panting. Then at a word from the king they began to climb gingerly down into the water, now red with blood, its mud churned by the horses, and started to pull the Sloronian knights clear. Helmets were wrenched off and heavy breastplates discarded. Amongst the battered bodies was found the Duke D’Urbin whose magnificent armour quickly denoted his high status. He was dragged clear and hauled up onto the bank. Bruised, soaked and shivering with cold, fear and humiliation, he was still alive. The King of Sloronia’s brother and commander–in-chief was worth, literally, a king’s ransom.

King Charles took a piece of parchment from his scrip, wrote a hasty command on it, reached into his overtunic for his Great Seal and endorsed the document. He handed it to the Earl of Bardsey.

‘Take this to the enemy. It acknowledges the end of the battle.’

Chapter 19

A YELLOW PLUME

King Charles and Peter had begun to trot down towards the brook when, from above and to the left of them, they saw Ferdinand le Gray cantering down. His medallion, with the prince's crest of a hound, was swinging from his neck.

'The freelances have attacked from the left flank,' he gasped. 'The prince requests your assistance, sire.'

King Charles turned his horse and, seeing a squadron of knights returning from the bridge, ordered them to follow. Ferdinand led the way back up the slope and towards the forest.

The party plunged into the trees. They could hear the sound of battle a little further on. Guided by the crash of fighting they pushed on and came upon a confused scene. As the king had predicted, the Duke D'Urbin had despatched a flanking attack under the Count di Montelucca. The freelances had run into Prince Rupert's party and now several hand-to-hand conflicts on foot raged in the broken snow among the saplings. The arrival of the king's party resolved matters for most of the Sloronian freelances threw down their weapons. Peter saw Knud. He was standing forlornly by his dead horse, a picture of dejection. He was no longer a swaggering warrior just a boy far from home with no idea of his future. Two or three mounted mercenaries made off in different directions through the trees. Amongst them was the Count di Montelucca in his yellow plumes.

'Rupert, get that wretch, di Montelucca. I'll handle this lot,' the king shouted.

Prince Rupert and Ferdinand remounted and set off after the count. The king, Peter and three other knights rode a little way further into the wood, to round up any others. They picked up a few stragglers and these were despatched to the Voravian lines as prisoners.

'Now let's see who we have captured. Bardsey should sleep easy for some years to come by the time we've ransomed all these nobles.' The king's light-hearted remark hid, Peter suspected, a sense of awe at the size of the victory.

They turned for home through the saplings. Shortly they emerged into a small clearing and, to one side, saw a figure bending over a fallen knight. The king rode over and, at his approach, the kneeling figure turned his head. It was Brother Simon.

The king dismounted, handed Stang's reins to Peter, and went over.

'May I help, Brother?' he asked.

'Have you any wine, sire? I need to remove this man's hand.'

'Peter, ride quickly to my tent and bring back a flask of wine. It is our quartermaster. Sir Hugh is an old comrade of mine. I cannot leave him now. You may leave Stang here. He will stay.'

The king removed his helmet, knelt down and gently lifted Sir Hugh Astley's head.

Peter spurred Belle down a path in the direction of the camp. He came up behind the prince who was on foot, holding his horse.

'Sire, I must pass. The king has sent me for some wine to deaden the pain of an amputation.'

The prince pulled aside into the scrub at the edge of the path, dislodging a shower of snow.

'Where is the king?' he asked.

'A little way back in a clearing, sire,' Peter answered and galloped off towards the camp.

As Peter rode along the ridge he could see the remains of the battle. Groups of prisoners were everywhere. Voravian soldiers were removing any valuables they could find. There was a huddle of nobility being guarded, as much for their own safety, as against their escaping. But the atmosphere was very different from the boisterousness that had followed the victory the previous autumn. The blood-smeared, bedraggled Voravians seemed overawed by the completeness of the victory and the scale of the slaughter. Peter looked across the valley, over the black gape of the brook with its gory contents, to the remains of the Sloronian army on the opposite ridge. Defeated, leaderless and without discipline, the survivors would now have to struggle back across that dreadful plateau, dying and broken in spirit to a cold welcome.

Even the weather seemed to mirror the scene as a great bank of snow-laden clouds was building in the west. Instead of jubilation in victory, a nervous gloom hung over the battlefield. The couplet that concluded one of Henry's sonnets floated into Peter's mind:

Ambition on our hopes is built.

But oft achieved, is soured with guilt.

He reached the king's tent where there was a crowd of senior officers and some of the Sloronian nobility. He forced his way through the throng and at last found a steward.

'His Majesty asks for a flask of wine.'

The steward returned with a flask, mounted a horse and the two of them cantered back towards the forest, Peter leading the way.

As they neared the clearing they came across the prince. He had with him Ferdinand and a prisoner, all mounted. It took Peter a minute to realize they had captured the Count di Montelucca.

They rode into the clearing. The snow had been heavily trampled. Over to one side lay King Charles. He was still alive but was bleeding from a gaping wound in his neck. The blood ran into a fast-widening crimson pool in the snow.

Brother Simon was crawling towards the king, his tunic stained from a wound. Sir Hugh Astley had fallen back and lay motionless.

The steward and Peter raced over to the monarch and leapt from their saddles.

'Help me unbuckle his armour,' the steward called, 'then go back for help.'

With difficulty, for King Charles was unable to move much, they managed to remove his breastplate, his collar and his gorget. They could see that the wound was deep and ragged.

As soon as he could, Peter remounted and set off for the camp. As he cleared the forest edge he caught up with the prince, Ferdinand and the count.

'The king is wounded, sire. We need help.'

'Conduct this prisoner to the camp.' The prince commanded Ferdinand and turned his horse to accompany Peter.

By the time the group reached the clearing another five or six knights, all aghast at hearing of the king's injury, were assembled. They were questioning a soldier.

'I comes into this 'ere dell. An' I sees the king an' he's bent over like, an' I could see as 'ow he were bad. An' I also sees this 'ere man on a 'orse. He were galloping away.'

'Who was he, soldier?' one of the knights asked.

'I doesn't know his name, sir. But I sees him when this war began. He were the leader of them freelances. He 'ad this 'elmet with yeller feathers on it.'

The steward held Stang by his reins. With much difficulty, for the king, even when relieved of most of his armour, was still a heavy man, the company lifted him onto his old horse. A knight stripped off his armour and mounted behind the king to steady him. Peter led Stang back through the trees.

By now the news of the terrible turn of events had spread throughout the army. Knights and soldiers began to file back up the slope.

When they arrived at the king's tent they gently lifted him down and laid him on a litter. It was apparent he was slipping away. A priest was called.

When he arrived he, the prince and Peter knelt by the dying monarch.

'I was struck down by Montelucca. I saw his helm, a yellow plume,' the king whispered.

He lay for a few minutes whilst the priest murmured a prayer. Then he turned to Peter and smiled gently at him.

'Peter, look after Lucy.'

'I will, sire, with my life.' Peter was unashamedly weeping.

The king managed a tiny smile. 'I fear I shall miss my rabbit stew.'

The tent filled with the captains and generals. The Duke of Flanders, tears streaming down his war-weary face, took the king's hand and pressed it to his lips. He was speechless with grief. Sir Walter hung back. He was no noble but as the nation's greatest general, others watched to take their cue from him.

There was another pause. The king struggled to speak and a thin trickle of blood seeped from his lips.

The prince approached, bent down and asked. 'Where is the Great Seal? That I may have the authority to govern in your absence?'

The king said nothing.

The prince repeated his request.

'I have given it to my most trusted friend,' the king spoke his last words.

The prince straightened his back. He stepped outside the tent. The fine weather had passed. The dark snow-laden cloud moved across the sun. The

Prince strode forward. Standing with Ferdinand was the Count di Montelucca. He had his back to the company by the tent and was speaking, in a friendly way, to his captor who held the yellow-plumed helm.

The prince went up to the count and, drawing his short-sword, seized di Montelucca by his hair. He dragged his head back and, shouting 'murderer', slit the count's throat.

The count fell sideways into Ferdinand, knocking the helm from Ferdinand's hands. It fell into the blood-soaked snow, its gorgeous yellow plumes rapidly turning crimson.

The prince turned round to face the astonished assembly.

'I could not bear to see the killer of our great King just standing there joking. Justice has been done.'

He sheathed his sword.

'Summon the generals to my tent, Sir Walter. We must make haste to the capital. The weather looks ever more threatening.'

Peter, shaking with grief, made his way towards his tent. He met Henry who put his arm round Peter's limp shoulders.

Suddenly Peter remembered Sir Hugh Astley and Brother Simon. Action was the best cure for sorrow, as his mother used to say when he was a child.

'Come with me, Henry. There are two wounded men in the forest. One is dear Brother Simon. We must help them.'

They mounted their horses and set off through the falling snow for the clearing where the good

King had been struck down.

They arrived to find the scene transformed by the new snowfall, but over to one side was a heap that could only be a man. They approached with dread and Peter dismounted. He scraped the snow from the body to reveal Sir Hugh. He was dead. A great gash across his throat had ended his life.

Peter looked up at Henry.

'He was killed at the same time as the king, by the same man. Where is Brother Simon? When I last saw him he looked badly injured.'

They made a desultory attempt to find the friar, but the fast falling snow hid any tracks. After a while, they decided to return to the camp.

That afternoon the army began its sad journey back to Nieuport. The body of King Charles lay in a cart. Stang was tethered to its tailboard.

Ferdinand sought Peter out.

'Tragic end to a fine king,' he observed, then added, 'Looks like your days in the sun are finished. It'll be back to behind the counter in your shop, I fear. Well, you should be much more at home there, eh?'

Now that Peter no longer had the patronage of the monarch it would appear that he had retracted his hand of friendship. Le Gray walked slowly away shaking his head.

Peter had to admit that this was the likely outcome, but one question kept surfacing in his mind. What had the king meant? Did 'take care of Lucy' mean he would have liked to see Peter and Lucy as man and wife? The king had told his father years ago that he had not the status to woo the princess, but now it seemed that perhaps the king had relented on his deathbed. Did he dare to think so?

Part Two

*

Crown and Sceptre

Princess Lucia of Voravia

'Never was anything great achieved
without danger.'
Niccolò Machiavelli

Chapter 20

ELSPETH

There came a tap at her door. Lucy pushed Henry's poem into the drawer of her desk.

The Duke of Flanders entered. He was filthy from having ridden hard and his face was contorted with agony.

He did not have to say a word. Lucy knew the worst.

She felt as if she had been struck with unimaginable force in her stomach. She felt physically sick. The man who had been the centre of her life, who had nurtured her, schooled her in the craft of leadership and had given so completely of his love, had been taken from her. Yet she had always known that something like this was a possibility. Ever since she could remember, her father had been at risk. He had, in a long reign and by judicious use of arms abroad and good government at home, built Voravia from just one of dozens of little nations into a power in Europe. But it had meant numerous campaigns to defend his country's independence. At the end of each the sense of relief at his safe return had always been tinged with fear that the next war would end tragically.

The awful emptiness seemed to crush her. She felt drained of all substance. It was as if her body were but a shell; her heart broken and wrenched from within her. She was utterly alone; her father, the anchor of her life, was gone. But it was even more than this. Their love, not only for each other but for their nation, had bound them together in a mutual cause. There was so much she wished she had discussed with him. There was so much she wished she had said to her dear, kind papa. Had she ever told him how much she loved him? Yet she did not burst into tears. Even in her desolate hour of grief she knew she must behave as the heir to the throne should. Her father would expect no less of her.

She turned to the duke, now her closest adviser, 'Flanders, what am I to do?'

'My lady, I've been thinking of little else as I rode to you. You have lost your father. Nothing, nothing can compare to your loss, but I can feel a little of your grief. I've lost my childhood friend, my brother in arms and Voravia too has lost her father. Your terrible grief is shared by thousands. You must, on behalf of all of us, your subjects, purge our sorrow, made all the more poignant by its happening at the hour of triumph. You must try to express in your demeanour the sorrow of the ordinary people of our land. Do you think you can do this?'

'I will try.'

'I know you will. Next you must rule. You carry a burden so great a strong man would quail at it, but I believe that within your slight frame beats the royal blood of your father.' Flanders paused to collect himself. Lucy could see the old warrior was fighting back his tears. He wiped his nose on his sleeve. 'Your father won a victory so great that our nation's safety is guaranteed for many years. Our borders may be secure, but there is always much to do to ensure our citizens live in peace and happiness. You will have the support of all good men and women. There is nothing, Princess, nothing I would not do for you, my sovereign and the daughter of my friend. You have only to ask.'

Only after the duke had left, did Lucy allow herself to weep.

The day of the funeral, February 12th 1535, dawned cold and wet. At ten o'clock the great bell of St. Stephano's cathedral began its solemn tolling and a small procession left the main gate of the castle and began its slow journey through the rain-swept streets of Nieuport.

At its head came the Duke of Flanders dressed in black and riding his warhorse. He was followed by the bier with the king's coffin lying upon it and his helmet, sword, crown and one wreath of wild spring flowers resting on the coffin lid. Behind the coffin, Stang was led by a groom. Fitted into the stirrups were the king's boots, reversed. Then, on foot and wearing a simple black shift, came the fifteen-year-old Queen Lucia, bareheaded. Behind her a troop of knights marched in sombre dress to the slow beat of a single drum and behind them Prince Rupert of Heinz-Coburg and his son and daughter, the Earl of Tuscade and Lady Barbara, rode in a closed carriage.

The prince had suggested that Lucy dress and bear herself as a monarch and ride in a closed carriage but she had decided that the best way she could follow the duke's advice would be to behave as one of her most humble subjects would at the death of a parent. Furthermore it suited her mood the better.

The streets were lined with sorrowful citizens, many sobbing. The sight of the brave, drenched, slight figure of their new sovereign stirred men as well as women. Some moved forward shyly to offer her bunches of snowdrops.

As she passed the Salts' shop, Peter stepped up to her.

'Be brave, I'm here if you ever need me. Be brave as Belle.'

She turned an exhausted, rain and tear-streaked countenance to him and gave a tiny smile at the remembrance of happy days, 'I know. I know you will.'

Stricken with grief as she was, Lucy was able to realize that her girlhood days were finished. With the death of King Charles, she was now the nation's head. She was faced with a choice. Either she could retreat into the frivolous life of the court, pass all decisions to her elders and be a pampered figurehead, or she could step into her father's shoes and devote her life to Voravia. As she felt the wave of affection from the crowds towards her, her decision was made. She straightened her back and set her jaw. She would be a monarch in her father's mould. By God, she would!

After the funeral service, conducted by a resplendent Archbishop Gregory, the new queen returned to the palace in her uncle's carriage. No sooner had they pulled up at the main door to the residential wing of the castle than the prince suggested they call a meeting of the council since all members were present in the capital.

There were eight members. Since King Charles had invited Lucy to attend council meetings as an observer for the previous six months she was familiar with the members. The archbishop and Flanders she had known since childhood. Like Flanders, the Duke de Guize, who boasted the impressive title of Lord of the Isles, and the Earl of Flytte were both aristocrats from ancient Voravian houses. Flytte was, in some complicated fashion, a relative of the Prince. In stark contrast were the Earl of Bardsey, the nation's treasurer, and Sir Thomas Paal, the governor general of the Company of Merchant Adventurers into Byzantium and Muscovy. They were what her father referred to as the New Men of Voravia. They had made their money by enterprise rather than inheritance. The prince took the chair.

Lucy examined this man who had stepped into the role of leader. He certainly looked the part, with his stern, calm, almost haughty demeanour. Although five years older than her father, in many ways, he appeared younger. Unlike the duke who, as had her father, preferred old well-worn clothes, the prince was immaculate. He was almost a dandy, carefully shaven with a neatly trimmed beard and doubtless he and his clothes were fastidiously washed. He had placed a small nosegay on his desk.

'Our first task is to negotiate the ransom of the Duke D'Urbin and the other Sloronian nobles. The Dark Tower is overflowing with prisoners. I'd like to suggest that we send our two wisest councillors on this important mission accompanied by Sir Walter Martley. Would the Duke of Flanders and the Earl of Bardsey be willing to represent us? I am sure the Sloronians will not intimidate the duke, rather the other way round. The earl, with his grasp of finances, will ensure the best possible deal is done and the presence of Sir Walter will remind the Sloronians that Voravia has the finest tactical soldier in Europe.'

On their visits around the realm her father had often remarked on the mutual dislike between prince and duke so Lucy wondered how Flanders would react to this suggestion. He was clearly astonished to be addressed so fulsomely by a man who, she suspected, loathed him.

'Of course, Prince. We should be able to negotiate from a position of great strength,' the duke replied with good grace.

Lucy felt, for the first time that dreadful day, a lightening of spirit. The prince had offered an olive branch to his enemy and the duke had accepted it. Could this mean that one of the problems she had been worrying about was on the way to being solved?

The earl however raised a problem. 'This mission is likely to take a few weeks. I'm worried I ought to be here, in Nieuport, to bring up to date the records so I may see the state of the nation's finances.'

The prince replied, 'I agree that this will need doing but, if the earl will let my son have a list of the documents you will need, I will see that they are ready for you on your return. Furthermore I'm confident that, with the strength of our representatives and the weakness of the Sloronian position, the ransom you obtain will more than balance the books.'

The duke turned to Lucy and said, 'Your Majesty, have we your permission to undertake this task?'

Lucy, who had begun to feel her presence was being completely ignored, replied with a smile, 'Your grace, you do indeed have my permission and let me wish you and your colleagues the best of fortune.'

'You are very gracious, my lady. You may count upon us all, as your most loyal servants, to do everything to aid you in the government of your land.'

Lucy had learnt over the years of mixing with many a tough fighting man that they often had a romantic soul and that youth and beauty spoke to this part of their character. As she resolved not to waste this power, she realised that she was already beginning to enter the politics of ruling.

So two days later the duke and his party left.

That evening the prince called upon Lucy.

'I am sure you are aware, Princess, that all the kings of Voravia are buried at the Abbey of Voravine.'

Lucy nodded

'I am thinking that perhaps you could visit the abbey and ask for the arrangements to be made for the interment of your father, one of Voravia's greatest kings. It may help distract you from your grief.'

'I will. You are right, Prince. Thank you.' Lucy had been feeling almost suffocated by the formality of the days since her father's death.

'You should travel in mourning, but in style. I have appointed my daughter, the Lady Barbara, to be one of your ladies-in-waiting. Lady Barbara will, I know, be able to help you in matters of etiquette. They are so important for someone in your position.'

'I thank you, Prince, but I assure you that I shall certainly take my maid, Elspeth, on my visit.'

'Elspeth is, no doubt, a good and loyal maid, but I think you should now be looking to, how shall I say, a more high-bred companion.'

'I shall not abandon Elspeth. That is my final word on this matter. However I am happy to visit Voravine.'

The next day, Lucy, the two ladies-in-waiting and Elspeth set out in two coaches for the abbey in the hills above Nieuport.

The weather was overcast, the countryside sodden from the melted snow and the almost continuous rain that followed it. Yet the further she moved away from the capital and in particular the prince, the more her spirits rose. It was difficult to say exactly why she feared the man. He was polite, almost ingratiatingly so, but she felt he had no sincerity. Her father, she knew, had never entirely trusted him, preferring the advice and company of others like his old friend the Duke of Flanders and his Treasurer, the Earl of Bardsey.

The prince's daughter, Lady Barbara, who, Lucy suspected, had been appointed mainly to spy upon her, travelled in the second coach with Lady Elizabeth Clovis, her other lady-in-waiting. No doubt they were gossiping about the scandals that swirled around the small number of noble families that made up the aristocracy of Voravia. Lucy looked across at Elspeth and smiled to think that she was apparently, and rather annoyingly, the object of Peter's chivalrous support. Well, he could do a lot worse.

Elspeth was six months older than Lucy. Her mother had been Lucy's wet nurse and the two of them had shared the same breast. Why, Lucy thought, we are almost sisters. She was a typical, comely country girl with the healthy complexion of a farmer's daughter. Below her broad brow and sandy eyebrows she had apple-green eyes, a nose with a tilt to it and a wide, generous mouth. When she smiled her cheeks dimpled and her pink tongue could be seen in the small gap between her two front teeth. A mop of curls, the colour of burnished copper, surrounded her freckled features. She was finding it difficult to adjust to the change in Lucy's status and, if Lucy were honest, it was quite pleasant to still be addressed as Mistress Lucy. She would much prefer Elspeth as a companion than the two noblewomen in the other carriage. But, there was a problem, well there were several, but one in particular.

'Elspeth, I've made a decision,' Lucy announced and lent forward, 'I'm going to teach you to read and write.'

'I am sure you could, Mistress, I mean Your Majesty, but I think I've not the wit to learn. Them letters look very complicated and what use would it be if I could read them?' Elspeth's cheery face had a worried expression on it.

'Well, for one thing, it would give you a better chance of making a good marriage.' Lucy laughed. She knew that Elspeth dreamed of a handsome young knight sweeping her away to live in some romantic castle. 'I was talking to a very good-looking young man not so long ago and he told me that he had just had a fight as your champion. I can tell you I was quite jealous but, I'm afraid, I stood no chance against your looks.'

'Oh Mistress, please don't tease me.' Elspeth had gone quite pink. There was a bit of a silence and Lucy watched Elspeth's smile as she drifted away into her reverie. Then she leaned forward. 'Who was it?'

'Ah, he promised me to secrecy but I'm sure he will be even more in love with you if he knew you would make a suitable wife for him. So, Elspeth, you really do need to read. It's not just so you can catch this handsome young man, but that, when the two of you are living in his great castle, you'll be able to manage his affairs when he is away fighting.'

Lucy could sense Elspeth was in a turmoil of excitement. 'Well, mistress, I shall learn, and when I can say my letters will you tell me his name?'

'Oh that's too easy for a quick brain like yours. But I am sure that soon he will send you a love letter and you'll not only be able to read it but write a response.'

'Oh, I will, I will. When do we start?'

'Now', said Lucy, 'well not just now, for I see we have arrived at a tavern where, I believe, we will take our midday meal.'

The two coaches drew up outside a roadside inn and the coachman helped Lucy and the two ladies-in-waiting descend. Elspeth had to jump down unaided.

Lady Barbara went in and demanded a private room and the tavern keeper, recognising quality when he saw it, bustled into the kitchen and dragged his protesting wife out. One glance at the three noble ladies convinced her that she should show them to the best parlour.

'Elspeth, you will eat in the public room,' Lady Barbara said in a tone she must have inherited from her father.

Elspeth bobbed a slightly cheeky curtsy and disappeared into the main room of the tavern.

Lucy, Lady Barbara and Lady Elizabeth were served a prim meal of cold ham, salt beef and a thin, sour white wine in a cold, damp backroom. It was eaten in almost complete silence. Towards the end, when Lucy could no longer bear both the frigidity of the room and the company, she excused herself and, after a visit to the closet, looked into the public room. She found Elspeth having a fine time in front of a huge fire with a party of farmers and their wives. Elspeth looked up, saw her mistress and hastily made her excuses.

'You seem to have had a rather better and warmer meal than we did judging by your smiles.'

'They was so kind, mistress, I mean my lady. They gave me two mugs of mulled wine and a pint of beer and some tasty cheese and some silverbrord that them farmers were taking to market. I could not finish all the beer.'

The journey continued, now beginning to climb into the mountains. There were patches of snow as they got higher. Elspeth's intention to start her lessons came to nothing as she very soon fell asleep.

They arrived at the abbey as the last of the daylight faded and were shown to clean pleasant rooms in the hospital.

A simple but filling meal of bread, salt fish and sparkling mountain water sent the party to bed. Elspeth prepared Lucy for the night and left.

Lucy said her prayers, asking God for His guidance in her rule. Then, before climbing into her bed, looked out of the window. The clouds had drifted away and the stars shone on the wooded landscape around the ancient abbey and the thin layer of snow. It was a beautiful night. She got into bed and snuggled beneath the rugs and felt a delicious sense of contentment. She smiled at Elspeth's enthusiasm and her uncomplicated life and drifted off into a deep sleep.

Chapter 21

THE EARL OF TUSCADE

It took three days for Lucy and the abbot to make the arrangements for the interment of King Charles' body in the vault at the abbey. Her relationship with her two ladies-in-waiting did not improve. Lucy suspected that her confiding more in Elspeth than in them constituted an insult to their status.

The weather was drier for the return journey but the party did not arrive back much before sunset. Lucy decided to speak to the prince the following morning. She requested Lady Barbara to ask him to attend her at midday.

She was seated at her desk in a businesslike way when the prince entered. After a brief formality of greeting she told him that everything had been successfully arranged.

The prince nodded and then he began to pace up and down the room with his hands clasped behind him and a deferential ingratiating smile on his thin lips but his dark eyes were hard.

'My dear Lucia,' he began, 'the council met three days ago to consider the running of the kingdom.'

'I was not there. I should have been.'

'Princess, please do not interrupt me. It was agreed that, as you are still but a child, a regent should be appointed to govern until you come of age in three years time. The council duly appointed me regent and, as such, all powers of government are vested in me as protector. I know this will come as something of a shock but you must understand that Voravia or, to my knowledge, any other European nation, has ever been ruled by a queen.'

'But I was not at that meeting; nor were the duke or the earl.'

'That is true. The duke and the earl were away on vital national business and, well, the very reason for appointing a protector, means that it was felt your presence would be, how shall I say, inappropriate.'

'I demand a full meeting of the council. Send for the duke and the earl.'

'My dear, that is impossible. They are by now many miles away. Now I suggest you retire to your dayroom. You must be tired from your exertions. Let me assure you, you will have all the privileges of your station without the needless worries that, I'm afraid, always accompany power. Now, I have work to do so will bid you good day.'

The prince walked briskly out of the room, leaving Lucy distraught.

Lucy sat for a few minutes turning over the change in events the last few minutes had wrought. Everything about the prince's words was worrying. If only the duke were here. But she knew he must be at least three days' riding away and every moment he would be further off.

There came a knock at her door and a footman opened it.

'The Duke of Flanders, Your Majesty,' he announced.

In swept the duke.

'Flanders,' Lucy cried out and rushed over to the soldier. 'How did you know I needed you?'

'I'd not been gone a day when I received news from the archbishop that there had been a council meeting at which the prince had received powers to be appointed regent. I realised that I'd been tricked into leaving court. Where is that blackguard?'

'He's only just left. He said I was too young to govern, is that so Flanders?'

'Not with me and all your subjects to help you, you most assuredly are not. You will make a damn sight better ruler than that dreadful uncle of yours.'

Lucy was about to reply when there came another knock on the door. It swung open and, as the footman was about to announce the prince, the man himself, followed by his son, the Earl of Tuscade, and four of his retinue forced their way into the room.

'Flanders, I was informed that you had abandoned your important mission on behalf of the nation and returned, unannounced, to Nieuport, no doubt to exercise your famous tact and cool reasoning in matters that do not concern you.'

'Don't you start patronising me you smooth-talking schemer. I'm told the Council met in my absence and agreed to your assuming the powers of regent and protector. Is this true?'

'Indeed, sir, it is. The vote was five to one, a clear majority.'

'Five to one was it? I take it the archbishop was the one honest man. Who were the other five?'

‘The Duke de Guize, the Earl of Flytte, Sir Thomas Paal, the Earl of Tuscade and myself,’ the prince responded.

‘The Earl of Tuscade, your son. He is not a member of the council. What the hell was he there for?’

‘You did not allow me to explain. In view of the age of the queen and the fact that she had absented herself, not unreasonably I should add, to make arrangements for the burying of the late king, my brother, it was felt that her place on the council should be taken by the earl. I have to say his contribution to our deliberations was very useful.’

Lucy looked at the earl, her cousin. She had not seen him for three or four years. His appearance had not improved. In boyhood he had been overweight with a drooping right eye but now his body seemed almost grotesquely stout. And not only his body, but his nose seemed to have swollen as well. Small broken blood vessels around his eyes showed purple against his pasty skin. He was dressed in a green jerkin whose silver buttons strained over his paunch. He gave a simpering smile and put his gloved hand to the hilt of his sword, one certainly more suited to ceremony than fighting.

‘And just what was his contribution?’ The duke was purple with anger.

‘Well, given the rather awkward dilemma we find ourselves in - a very young heir to the throne but the need for firm government - it was suggested that a solution would be for the Princess Lucia and the earl to be betrothed. In this way I, as regent, would by allied by marriage to the princess, as heir.'

'What?' roared the duke, 'King Charles' daughter - my sovereign - marry Tuscade! Never will I allow that.'

'I shall not marry anyone until I wish to,' Lucy declared, panic swirling through her head. 'Even the humblest girl in our kingdom may choose whom she weds.'

'So far as I'm concerned the common people may wed, or should I say mate, with whomsoever they wish. They are little better than animals. The nobility is a different matter,' snapped the prince.

'I will not have my people referred to as animals. They are all equal before the law and in my estimation. Many are far better than members of the nobility,' Lucy retorted.

'Well spoken, my lady. You may count on me, come what may. It shall not happen.'

'Flanders, you are in grave danger of overreaching yourself. The council has voted. Even had you and Bardsey been present, the vote would have been decisive. Now, please leave this room.'

'I most certainly will not. Furthermore, I assume the council's decision was not sealed. Or have you found the Great Seal?'

'What makes you think the decision was not sealed?' the prince enquired.

'Everyone knows the Seal is missing. On my way to the castle I was told the Earl of Tuscade has placed a very large reward for its recovery.'

The prince spun round on his son.

'You fool, what were you thinking of? Are you completely incapable of doing anything sensible?'

'Your son is not only a drunken gambler, a whoremonger and a snivelling little coward who has never seen action, but he's a fool. You know all that to be true.'

Tuscade took a tentative step forward.

'You will retract those insulting and untrue words or I shall be forced to seek satisfaction.'

Lucy noticed that beneath the earl's deformed eye a violent tic was hammering. The earl lifted a gloved hand to try to stay the movement.

The duke gave a roar of laughter. 'And just what have you in mind, you strutting popinjay? Are you challenging me to a duel? Well, that would be one way of ensuring this preposterous marriage does not take place.'

Flanders began to remove his glove. The prince took a rapid step forward between Tuscade and the duke.

'Flanders, such a contest would be absurd. You are an experienced soldier. My son has not been able to gain such experience due to his…his unfortunate eyesight. It would be beyond your honour to take part in what would be so unequal a fight.' The prince tried to be conciliatory.

But the duke's anger was not going to be assuaged now.

'If I had not returned, God knows what would have happened. This sweet girl would have been married off to that oaf, just to cement your grip on power. Well, I shall ensure no such thing takes place. I shall resist your illegal usurpation of power with all my might. I should advise you both that I have three thousand men at my call.'

'Flanders, this is treason. You are refusing to accept the vote of the council. Furthermore, you are inciting a fellow council member to a duel. Unless you leave this room immediately, I will order your arrest here and now and your summary trial before me on high treason. Should you be found guilty you will be executed and your land and properties forfeit to the Earl of Tuscade. Do I make myself clear?'

The prince beckoned to the soldiers who stepped forward and seized the duke.

'Duke, please, say you didn't mean your words. Prince Rupert is trying to trap you.' Lucy was almost in tears.

'Your Majesty, thirty something years ago, at the coronation of your father, King Charles IV, I gave my oath to serve him and his successors. I have no intention of breaking that oath. I am no longer a young man. I shall, one day, with Christ's mercy, meet your father in paradise. I could never face my old friend and sovereign if I had broken my oath. I shall not retract. Let this usurper do his damnedest.'

'Take him away now. Incarcerate him in the Dark Tower. If necessary free one of the Sloronians,' the prince roared.

With great dignity the duke was marched from the room.

'The duke seems to set great store by the prospect

of his afterlife in heaven. Well, he'll soon know if his confidence is well placed,' the prince remarked. 'For myself, I prefer to concentrate on this life here, on earth.'

Lucy turned on the prince. 'Uncle Rupert, you cannot mean to execute the duke. You know he has a quick temper and speaks before he thinks but I'm sure he will realise his mistake once he has a chance to cool down. Please spare him. He is a good man and a great patriot. He was my father's best friend.'

'Best friend was he? I wonder if that makes him his most faithful friend. Your father said he had entrusted the Great Seal to his most faithful friend. Rather than offering rewards, I think we should put a little pressure on that hot-headed man. He's brave enough when it comes to being challenged by the earl here, but I wonder how brave he'll be when he is on the rack. When he feels his joints give, when his sinews begin to tear, when he smells the rupturing of his bowels, then he will assuredly reveal the location of that seal. Son, come with me. The discussion of the wedding can wait until the princess is in a more cooperative frame of mind.'

The prince and the earl left the room. Lucy collapsed at her desk, her head in her hands.

Chapter 22

THE DARK TOWER

‘*Be brave, I am here if ever you need me,’* Peter’s words.

‘I have no one to turn to,’ thought Lucy, ‘except my old school-friend. I’ll go to him and his family.’

She rose and walked over to the door. She opened it and was confronted by the Lady Barbara.

‘Princess, is there anything you want?’ Lady Barbara seemed to have grown several inches taller, such was the veiled threat in her manner.

‘I was thinking of taking a walk. I would like to visit the cathedral,’ Lucy could think of no better excuse.

‘I shall accompany you. Of course, we cannot have the queen-to-be walking the streets of Nieuport alone. That would be far too dangerous. I will just tell my father that we will be going to St Stephano’s. He might well send my brother along. I know the Earl of Tuscade would dearly like to act as your escort.’

‘No, I’ve quite changed my mind. Send for my maid, will you?’

Lucy, shaking with fear, closed the door and returned to her seat.

A tap at the door announced Elspeth.

‘Come in and close the door, Elspeth. I want to change the way I wear my hair. I want to have it up. Can you manage that?’ Lucy said this in a loud voice and gave a vigorous nod of her head.

‘Yes, mistress,’ Elspeth replied in what Lucy hoped was a loud enough voice so that Lady Barbara would hear it.

Lucy beckoned Elspeth over to the window, as far away from the door as possible, and said in a whisper, ‘Elspeth, I’m in danger. I believe the prince and his family are determined to seize power. My friend the Duke of Flanders is arrested and may very likely be executed. Sir Walter is far away and I have no one to turn to.’

‘You have me, my lady. I will die for you. Oh I know I am no reader but I have a heart as strong as anyone. I isn’t scared of horrible witches like that Lady Barbara and if that there prince so much as lays a finger on you he‘ll have me to fight.’

‘They want me to marry the prince’s son, the Earl of Tuscade. He’s a horrible man.’

‘You want me to kill the earl?’ Lucy could quite believe Elspeth would not hesitate.

‘No, well, not just yet. But at the first opportunity we must get out of this castle. I know somewhere we could hide.’

There came a brisk tap at the door and it was flung open by Ferdinand le Gray, the prince’s squire. Ferdinand was dressed in the height of fashion, with a doublet of silk and around his neck a medallion of a black dog.

‘Princess Lucia, the prince feels that, for your own safety, you should no longer reside in these near-public rooms. There is a rumour of a plot to assassinate you. We have reason to suspect followers of the Duke of

Flanders are involved. I am to escort you to the Dark Tower as the safest place.'

'No, that is quite wrong,' shouted Elspeth and flung herself at Ferdinand.

The squire was completely taken aback by the blow and fell into the arms of the three soldiers he had with him.

'Take them both to the Tower,' he ordered, 'the top floor rooms.'

'I demand my books, my quills and my paper.' Lucy spoke with as much dignity as she could muster.

'You have a chest?' Ferdinand asked. 'Tell that little vixen of a maid of yours she is to place some of your clothes in it and your books and, I suppose, a change of attire for the woman herself. She has ten minutes.'

Two soldiers carried Lucy's chest across the main courtyard of the palace to the Dark Tower, the most ancient part of the great castle. Lucy and Elspeth followed with Ferdinand bringing up the rear. They were met at the doorway to the tower by a low-browed, leather-clad retainer.

'Conduct the princess to her apartment, Vladimar,' Ferdinand ordered

They mounted the narrow stairway. On each floor there were posted gaolers, for this was the prison for men of high rank and now it was full of Sloronian nobles awaiting their freedom upon a suitable ransom being paid. After climbing past four floors they arrived at a heavy oak door and Vladimar produced from his jacket an enormous key. He inserted it in the lock, turned it and threw open the door.

The room was surprisingly pleasant. Situated immediately below the top of the tower it had quite a high ceiling. There was a fireplace with a pile of dry wood and kindling and two large windows, each with shutters. There were three vertical bars to each window but no horizontal ones, so there was not the impression of a cell. Lucy believed that in former days, before the more recent additions to the castle, it had been the solar, a room often used by the queen and her ladies. There was a small truckle bed, a desk, a prie-dieu with a padded hassock for Lucy to kneel at to say her prayers, two chairs, a wardrobe, a bookcase and a washbasin and jug, both of fine pottery, on a table One window looked onto the central courtyard of the castle, the other looked out over the city. To the left of this window, in the far corner, was a door into the privy.

Vladimar told the soldiers to put the chest on the floor and when they had left he told Elspeth to open it and unpack.

Elspeth took out Lucy's clothes and hung them in the wardrobe. Then she began to arrange Lucy's books in the case.

'Don't hold with all this 'ere reading and writing,' said Vladimar. 'Can't see the point of it. Only 'urts yer eyes. Still if yer goin' to be cooped up in 'ere all yer days I suppose it will give you something to do.'

Lucy spun round. 'What do you mean, cooped up here all my days?'

'Just that, miss. Prince's orders. You've to stay right 'ere in this room and no visitors without 'is permission. So it seems we three will 'ave to get to know each other if we're going to 'ave to put up with each other's company.'

'I must be brave, I will not cry,' she said to herself, noting that Elspeth had run into her room. Lucy could hear her sobbing.

Lucy rose, nodded to Vladimar, and went down the short passage to the left of the privy to another door with a key in it. She pushed open the door to Elspeth's chamber.

Elspeth's room had a small window high in the outside wall. Her furniture consisted of a bed similar to Lucy's, a chair and a small table with a pewter basin and wooden pail for water.

Lucy sat on the bed, put her arms round her maid and stroked her hair. 'We'll be all right, Elspeth, you'll see. Now this very afternoon we will start on your reading.'

The lesson was not a success. Neither girl was in the mood and the arrival of the evening meal and the fading of the light at last brought an end to their efforts.

'If we stick together, Elspeth, we will get through the next few days and then I'm sure the duke will soon have us out. Now help me undress and then we'll be much more cheerful in the morning.' Lucy hoped her tone did not convey her fears.

Elspeth prepared her young mistress for the night then retired to her own room.

Lucy sat down on the bed. It creaked under her weight. The mattress was a sack of straw. It shifted back to reveal the structure of the bed. Its simple wooden frame of four vertical planks was held together with wooden pegs. Across the top edges of these planks were a series of slots and fitting into these slots was a long piece of rope threaded from left to right and back again to form a base for the mattress. It was a typical bed of the ordinary people, quite unlike the huge four-poster with its deep mattresses to which she had been accustomed.

She said her evening prayers at her prie-dieu and lay down on her humble bed. It was many hours before she dropped off to sleep.

For the next twenty days there was little change to the routine of Lucy and Elspeth's days. The weather became milder as March followed February. Vladimar would bring them their meals three times a day and Lucy spent much time either reading or teaching Elspeth to read. To start with she despaired of making any progress. Elspeth seemed to forget almost everything she had learnt the previous day. Vladimar did not help. He was constantly pouring scorn on the very idea. But one day Elspeth seemed to have crossed some invisible obstacle. She read a complete sentence without a pause, then looked up and began the next one. Lucy was almost as excited as her pupil.

As a further distraction Lucy decided to make a sundial on the south-facing window ledge. This was the window that looked out towards the roofs of

Nieuport. Below it was a great drop to the dried moat. Between the moat and the houses she could see the track from the stables that led to the lower gate and thence to the gallops along the river.

She would use the central bar as the gnomon. The first task was to locate south. She carefully observed the height of the sun and, when it was at its zenith, she made a scratch on the sill. Vladimar watched the experiment with interest and supplied Lucy with a sand timer to allow her to mark the hours. Of course she could only mark each hour after noon but reasoned that, once these were done, the gap between eleven and noon would be the same as between noon and one in the afternoon. She smiled as she thought how pleased William Salt would be at her scientific approach.

It was on the twenty-first day of the captivity that Vladimar arrived at midday limping.

'Whatever is the matter?' Lucy asked.

'I were kicked by a 'orse two days ago and the wound seems worse. I've tried putting 'oney and cow dung on it but 'tis no better,' Vladimar replied.

'Let me see it,' Lucy said. 'Sit down in the chair and take your shoe off.'

Vladimar sat down. Lucy could see he was in agony.

Lucy removed his shoe and hose to reveal a rough bandage, much discoloured. There was a dreadful smell. Lucy carefully peeled the bandage away from a suppurating wound. It had an angry red rim and beyond that the skin had a yellowish tinge.

Vladimar looked at his leg.

‘’Tis a bad wound I fear. The old lady at the tavern told me to use the ’oney and the cow dung, but it don’t seem to be doing no good.’

‘That’s just superstition. You were lucky she did no more harm.’

Lucy thought for a while. Then she got up, went across to her desk and drew a piece of parchment from a drawer. She found a quill and some ink. Then she wrote a letter to William Salt.

The bearer of this letter is my gaoler, Vladimar. He cannot read. I am imprisoned in the Dark Tower by Prince Rupert. Please do your best for Vladimar, he is a kind man. I will defray any costs.

Princess Lucia

She folded the letter and wrote: *To William Salt* on it.

‘Take this to the apothecary on Whitefriars Street. If any man can cure your leg it is he.’

Vladimar took the note.

‘The apothecary will be able to read it?’ he asked.

‘Naturally, Vladimar.’

Lucy went to her chest and took out a petticoat.

‘Cut it here.’ She indicated the hem.

Vladimar took out his dagger and slit the linen. Lucy ripped off a strip of material and fashioned it into a bandage and bound it round the wound, then she replaced the hose.

Vladimar put on his shoe and hobbled out of the room, pausing to lock the door. Lucy heard him start down the stairs.

Chapter 23

BROTHER SIMON

Peter, now no longer a squire, had returned to his parents' home. He had made the transition from a life at court to that of an apothecary's son remarkably easily. The worst losses were the absence of Lucy's company and of Belle, who was now back in the royal stables. He still dreamt of being able to tell Lucy of his love, which with every day of her absence, seemed to grow more enveloping.

'What is the matter?' William asked him.

Embarrassed to confess what the true reason was, Peter mumbled that he longed to be able to ride Belle. Once again, he had shied away from the truth at the last minute.

'Well, why don't you go and ask the head groom? I'm sure he would let you,' William suggested.

As he walked up towards the yard Peter could sense a sullen angry mood in the streets. He met an old friend of the Salts, a merchant who lived three houses down on Whitefriars, and asked him the cause.

'The Council has placed a tax on wool imports. It is a blatant means of assisting the rich landlords of Heinz-Coburg.'

'Heinz-Coburg? That's the prince's homeland, isn't it?'

'Yes, and its economy is dependent on sheep. The prince is the greatest landlord there. He is enriching himself at our expense. Thomas Paal tried to object on behalf of the Muscovy traders and others like me, and he's been thrown into jail for his pains. Of course the ordinary citizen is not too bothered by such matters. He should be, for the price of wool will rise. But, Master Peter, that is not the reason for the atmosphere today.'

'And what is that, sir?'

'Have you not heard? They have banned the St. Pelagius day festivities. King Charles never minded a few jibes at the royal family. Nor did the archbishop. Gave the people a chance to have a bit of fun. Those parades, with their masks, are a part of the common man's traditions. Now our new master knows they will mock him and that son of his.'

'Will there be trouble, do you think?'

'Could be, but the criers said they'd set the Palace Guard on anyone disobeying the order. I know our new queen is very young but I can't help wishing it were King Charles' daughter making the decisions. Still what can we do? Just have to make the best of things. Give my regards to your parents.' The merchant doffed his cap and moved off down the street.

Peter walked on up to the stables thinking that the change from the jovial King Charles to the severe Prince Rupert would mean a drearier Nieuport.

'I was wondering how long you'd be able to keep away from your love, young man.' Jack Farthing greeted him. 'Why, since no one else is giving her any exercise, 't'would be a good idea if you was to. Just you come up here whenever you like. You'll always be welcome. The lads always respects someone who rides well. An' the way you thrashed them two toffs did your reputation no 'arm. No 'arm at all.'

It took Peter almost three weeks to return Belle to her former level of fitness. One day, having rubbed her down, given her a couple of apples and walked back to the shop, he found a stranger hovering outside the door.

'Yes, sir, what may I do for you?' he enquired.

The man was of the lowest sort. His clothes were not much more than sacks and he had evidently travelled far and was exhausted.

'I was looking for Master William Salt, sir. Are you him?'

'No, he's my father. He's out at the moment. You look to be very tired. Please come in. Would you like some bread?'

The man nodded. They entered and Peter offered the visitor a seat. He fell into it.

When Peter had brought him a half loaf, an apple and a mug of beer, he asked what he wanted.

'My name is Robert Hawkins and me and the wife, we 'as a farm t'other side of the river.' He took a swig of his beer and a mouthful of bread. 'About a month ago there were a terrible battle near our place in the snow and, well, the next day some of us went up to the battlefield, to see if there was anything useful we could find.'

Peter nodded. He knew that a battlefield often yielded rich pickings and this one would probably do so more than most since the snow would have hidden much equipment and moreover both armies had left the scene so quickly.

'Anyways I never got there. I had not gone a mile before I came across this poor near-dead creature. He were a friar and he had a terrible wound in his neck. He were laying there in the snow. At first I thought he was dead but he sort of stirred a bit as you might say. Well, he being a man of God I could not just let him be, could I? So I half carried him, half dragged him back to our farm. Lucky he was a so light, more like a girl than a full-grown man.

'My missus, she cleaned up his wound, best she could and we got him to bed. Next day he seemed as if he would just give up and die but somehow he lasted. We got him to sip a little water and some milk, but sir, we never thought he'd live. Anyhow he did and then three days ago he managed to ask for William Salt here in Nieuport. I never been to Nieuport before but I knew I must try. So I sets out and three days it has taken me to get here, sleeping in the hedgerows.'

Peter's heart began to pound. 'Do you know his name, this friar?'

'Aye, 'tis Brother Simon.'

'Brother Simon! He's our friend and you say he's alive. That's wonderful.'

'Only just, sir. Every moment matters.'

Chapter 24

GANGRENE

They brought Brother Simon back and put him in Peter's room then made up a bed for Peter in the pantry. Abigail took charge of nursing the friar and slowly he began to gain strength as his dreadful wound healed.

One Friday, Peter was preparing a tincture of camomile when the door opened. He was astonished to see Vladimar hobble in.

'Why, hello Vladimar, what brings you here?'

'I've a note for the apothecary,' said Vladimar.

Peter unfolded the letter and read the short note.

'I must take this to my father. He has a sick man with him at the moment. Please wait. The note says your leg is bad so I think you should come through to the kitchen and sit down.'

Peter led Vladimar into the rear room and introduced him to Abigail.

Ten minutes later William came down from the sickroom.

'For the first time since he arrived here, Brother Simon is sleeping quietly. I believe we will save him yet. Now who have we here?'

'This is Vladimar from the castle. Princess Lucia has sent him with this note.'

Peter managed to turn his father so that he had his back to Vladimar when he read the note. Even so William gave a start when he read its contents.

He turned to Vladimar. 'You appear to have a

good and kind friend in the princess. She has asked me to make any charge for treatment to her. Now let me see the injury.'

Peter watched as William gently removed Lucy's bandage.

'It's as well you came when you did. In a few more days gangrene would have set in and it would have meant an amputation. Now, I am going to clean the wound and my Abigail will make a poultice to apply to it. You are not on any account to take the dressing off. You must return here tomorrow. We need to draw the poison from the blood.'

William turned to Peter. 'Go into the shop and bring me some clay of gypsum and a jar of witch hazel. Abigail, be so good as to let me have a small pan to warm the compound.'

Peter returned with the ingredients and a few minutes later William was wrapping the bandage round Vladimar's leg. He fixed it in place with a bronze pin.

'There, now you can return to your duties but remember; I must see you tomorrow.' William helped the gaoler to his feet.

That evening Vladimar brought Lucy and Elspeth their meal. He set it down politely on the table and said, 'Princess Lucia, you is as kind as you is beautiful. I can't thank you proper for sending me to the apothecary. I were wrong about this 'ere reading. I've been thinking that now Elspeth has learnt, could you teach me?' It was apparent he had been rehearsing his speech but it was none the less moving.

Lucy laughed. 'Well, I never thought that one day I'd become a teacher. My father gave me quite the wrong training.'

Vladimar began to say something then stopped.

'Oh, let us try! Elspeth, give Vladimar your letters. That is where we begin.'

So Lucy and Vladimar, sat side by side at her desk and Lucy explained that each letter represented a different sound. From ardent disbeliever in the wisdom of reading, Vladimar became the keenest of pupils.

For the following four days Vladimar visited the Salts' shop and both he and they were pleased to see that, first the inflamed flesh grew less fiery, and then the wound began to heal. He also began to make some progress with his reading.

It was on the fifth day, when he had just finished repeating his alphabet and the princess was finding a simple passage from her Bible to show him how the letters formed words, that he suddenly blurted out. 'Princess, I can't stay silent no longer. I am going to help you escape.'

Lucy looked up in astonishment.

'How, Vladimar? It would be enormous risk not only for me but most especially for you.'

'I'll bring in some of my sons' old clothes these next few days. I'll hide them on my person. Then you can escape, disguised as a boy. Please let me do this for you, I ain't done much good in my life, just let me do this one thing.' Then Vladimar added, 'I ain't dared tell you this, Princess Lucia, for fear of disturbing you, but I must. Three days ago the Duke of Flanders were beheaded, on the orders of the protector.'

'Why? Vladimar?'

'There were a march to demand 'is freedom. The soldiers attacked the marchers. The apothecary and 'is son were in the march but escaped injury, but several others were badly 'urt. The duke, they said, 'e 'ad organised the march, though he were in prison.'

Chapter 25

ESCAPE

'What!' cried Lucy, 'Oh, God, what is to become of us? They've killed a man who always, always put his country first. For what? I will tell you for what? For trying to stop the prince in his plans to take absolute power. We must, no, I must do something for our poor nation.'

She put her head in her hands and felt the tears well in her eyes, but she recognised that her anger was as strong as her sorrow.

'I am sorry to bear this terrible news, my lady, but now you see, I got to free you. You're the only hope we has. An' I must tell you something more, though if the prince learns of it, I'm a dead man. Some time ago, even afore the death of your good father, I were approached and asked to do away with you. I were promised a 'uge sum of money. Well, I could certainly do with the money, an', if you hadn't been such a pretty girl, well maybe I would've done it. Anyhows I said as 'ow me religious beliefs would not allow it and this man, he said he'd find someone who weren't so squeamish.'

'I can believe both parts of that, Vladimar, and I must thank you from the bottom of my heart. You are a good man.' Lucy's fury had steeled her will to fight.

'So, now you see, you must escape. All over the city, everywhere, people are asking where you are.

The protector's rule is 'ated. Please say yes.'

'I shall escape, provided Elspeth comes as well.'

'Of course she will. It will be easy to disguise you, Princess, as a boy. Your Elspeth, she 'as a more womanly sort of shape. We'll have to push 'er into my Jack's jerkin and breeches.'

In spite of her anger and distress, Lucy could not help smiling at the thought.

The next day Vladimar brought in a leather doublet and Lucy hid it in her chest. On the following day, shortly after having delivered a second larger doublet for Elspeth, he returned to announce the Earl of Tuscade.

It was apparent that Tuscade had made a great effort to make himself presentable. He was wearing a loose-fitting doublet of dark green wool embroidered with a floral pattern in pale green, his leggings were in black and he had on the most fashionable red leather shoes. He wore a large black floppy hat with a silver brooch of a prancing stag pinned in it. Over his doublet was a cloak in dark blue, lined with crimson silk and fastened at the neck with a silver clip. At his waist he wore his fine dress sword. He looked huge but soft.

Lucy was at her desk assisting Elspeth in reading a passage from her Bible. She had chosen the story about the daughter of Pharaoh discovering baby Moses in the bulrushes, one that she felt sure Elspeth would recognise.

'Cousin Lucia,' he began, 'may I ask you to dismiss your maid? I wish to speak with you in private.'

'No, you may not. You know as well as I that it would be most unseemly for me to receive you in private. Elspeth will stay.' Lucy turned a stern face to the wretched earl.

'Lucia, I was too precipitate when I asked you to consent to be my wife. It was too much of a shock for you. But now that you have had a week or two to consider matters and for the good of both our families, my father was hoping you would relent and agree to the match. And so was I,' the earl added.

Lucy noticed the tic had started below the earl's droopy right eye. She watched as he tried to quiet it with his finger.

'No, my mind is quite resolved, I will not marry anyone unless I love them.' Lucy's tone was not encouraging.

'But perhaps someone else has your heart,' Tuscade suggested.

'No, there is no one. My heart belongs to Voravia.'

The earl, clearly astonished by the reply, was stuck for a response.

'And what about you, Elspeth? Are you as chaste as your mistress?'

'Oh, no, I love lots of men,' the girl replied with a laugh.

'Perhaps, Earl, you are pursuing the wrong girl. Though, on second thoughts, I fear you would have too much competition in Elspeth's case. Everyone knows she has dozens of handsome young men seeking her hand.'

'Cousin, you mock me. Do you dislike me?'

'I am quite indifferent to you. It would pain me to see you trying to win me if I thought you really loved me. But I don't believe you do. You're driven, not by your heart, but by calculation. Neither of us would be happy yoked together. You would find it hard to be faithful and I would certainly be a poor wife. No, let us part as friends and family.' Lucy found slipping into the regal manner surprisingly easy.

The earl, having tried politeness and civility, decided that a more aggressive approach was called for. He rose, crossed to the seated princess and, placing a hand on each shoulder, dragged her round and stooped to kiss her. Lucy put both hands on his chin and pushed him away. The hot blast of his spirit-laden breath hit her nostrils.

The next moment the earl received a tremendous blow to the side of his head as Elspeth hit him with the heavy Bible.

He staggered sideways. Lucy could hardly believe it. Her immediate reaction was one of relief. Elspeth had saved her from, at the least, an embarrassing confrontation. But was there not a danger that a nobleman like Tuscade would be so affronted by the actions of a maid that he would find an opportunity to gain his revenge one day? Their escape became the more vital.

'I think it'd be better if you were to leave us now, before Elspeth does you some real harm,' said Lucy.

Tuscade leant against the wall. He was breathing hard and a tiny trickle of blood oozed from his lip.

His look at Elspeth was one of confusion and hatred. He shook his head as if in disbelief and left the room, slamming the door and locking it.

Over the following four days Vladimar built up a complete set of clothes for Lucy and Elspeth. He told Lucy that he had found somewhere for them to hide; a sister had a small farm about three hours walk from Nieuport. Once a week, on a Thursday, which was tomorrow, she brought produce in to market. His plan was that they would leave about an hour before dusk, reach the market as the stallholders were preparing to go back to their farms and Lucy and Elspeth, in their disguise, would pass through the gate on a cart.

At midday on the day of the escape, Vladimar delivered their meal and told them to be ready, dressed in their disguises, when he returned at five. He had let it be known that his sons were coming into the castle and he expected no trouble with the guards.

In a fever of excitement Lucy and Elspeth climbed into the clothes Vladimar had brought. Elspeth gathered up Lucy's long tresses and tucked them up under her cap. Lucy went round Elspeth arranging her rough working clothes so as to make her look as like a boy as possible.

The pair of them watched the shadow on the sundial creep towards the five o'clock line.

It slipped past it. Then they heard the key turn in the lock and, with pounding hearts, they prepared for the escape.

Chapter 26

THE PRIE-DIEU

For a second the door stuck as it often did, then it swung open to reveal Ferdinand le Gray. He was dressed in a bodice of plum with a surcoat of cherry, both in the finest silk. The surcoat was embroidered with silver filigree. Round his neck hung the badge of the prince. A short sword hung from the belt at his waist.

'So, what do I find? Two young men ready to flee their pleasant lodgings. Lest you are wondering where Vladimar is, I will tell you. He is dangling from a rope, his treacherous neck broken. He took a long time to go, but that is what a traitor deserves. I could have given the order for his legs to be pulled. That would have ensured a swift end. But I did not. He died in terrifying agony. I've been watching him these last weeks and it was obvious, to even the simplest of brains, that he was up to no good.'

Lucy, her hopes dashed and horrified at Ferdinand's cruelty, staggered back and clutched at the edge of the prie-dieu. Eventually she felt her heart slow.

'He was only driven by a desire to help me, not by any wish to harm the state. He is no traitor, Ferdinand,' Lucy said defiantly.

'Sir Ferdinand, please. And do not refer to Vladimar in the present tense, he is dead, do you understand? Quite dead. His widow will doubtless be forced into the gutter with her children. An example to anyone else who might think of stirring up trouble against the prince.'

'Sir Ferdinand? You have been knighted?' Lucy asked.

'Indeed, and what is more, I am now a member of the council. The prince knows who he can trust, and he has every reason to trust me. Incidentally, my knighthood, whilst welcome and much deserved, will shortly be surpassed by my being created Duke of Bellaire. For that is the price the prince has agreed to pay for the service I shall perform for him this evening. So sit down princess, whilst I let you know what is in store for the pair of you.'

Lucy remained where she was.

'I said sit down.' Ferdinand snapped.

Lucy took Elspeth's hand and sat in her chair at her desk. Sir Ferdinand took the heavy oak armchair and sat down. He stretched his legs out in a satisfied manner.

'Your maid has assaulted the Earl of Tuscade who, incidentally, will shortly be my brother-in-law. He will expect his revenge.'

'Your brother-in-law! Is he to marry your sister?' Lucy interrupted

'My sister marry that diseased wreck? Heaven forbid. No, I am to marry the Lady Barbara. We don't imagine the earl is very much longer for this world. He has a disgusting fistula on his right calf and rumour has it another has recently taken hold, appropriately, in his privy parts. It is conjectured he has this infection the Spanish have brought back from the New World.

However, that will not prevent his making your maid much regret her headstrong action. This very evening the earl, who is taking advantage of his father's absence to indulge his passion for wagering, intends to visit her here.' He paused then added, 'You and I, princess, will have the pleasure of listening as the earl indulges his desire for satisfaction.'

'He will have to fight for it,' Elspeth snapped.

'Oh the earl may be a coward and a debauched ruin, but he has a reputation for great daring - and not a little ingenuity - when it comes to dealing with a defenceless woman. He'll take much pleasure in indulging his fondness for inflicting pain. The earl intends to keep you imprisoned, not in these pleasant apartments you may be sure, for the remainder of what he terms your useful existence. Tuscade, who has never done a useful job in his entire life, has undertaken to be your sole gaoler. He may prolong your life longer than you would wish. Many a victim of his has welcomed an early death. Lonely and hungry you may be in your cell, but I doubt you will look forward much to his visits. Oh dear, you will assuredly pay a heavy price for your impudence. I almost feel sorry for you, you little slut.'

Elspeth's left hand flew to her mouth.

Lucy gripped her right hand tight. 'It will not happen, Elspeth. He is just trying to scare you.'

'Time will show,' Sir Ferdinand remarked lightly,

'Now, princess,' he continued and his voice took on a hard edge, 'I think you need to appreciate that Sir Walter is not the only man in the kingdom capable of making a coherent plan. The prince left four days ago accompanying the Sloronian nobles to meet the Earl of Bardsey and Sir Walter who are returning from their ransom mission to Sloronia.

'They have extracted a ransom for the Duke D'Urbin and the other nobles. It is a disappointing sum but still enough to ensure the prince has a full treasury. Sometime, during the return journey with the bullion, they will be met by the prince and a large party of his armed men. The earl and Sir Walter will be arrested and tried for their failure to extract more and it's likely they will be forfeit of their estates and executed. There is a strong possibility that one of them knows the whereabouts of the Great Seal. Without it, the prince is having difficulty in making the county sheriffs do his bidding. If either of them knows its whereabouts, I have little doubt that, with suitable persuasion, he will tell. If only to obtain a dignified death.'

Lucy rose and stood hand in hand with Elspeth.

'This is impossible. Have you and the prince gone mad? The council will never allow it. Sir Thomas Paal, he owes everything to my family, he will oppose such an action.'

'Sir Thomas? He's a jumped-up tradesman. What he and his partners in the Merchant Adventurers want, above all, is stability so they can pursue their money-grubbing little lives. That is why he voted for the appointment of the prince as protector. However, he has recently taken to objecting to some of the sensible arrangements the prince has instituted as regards taxation and is now a fellow prisoner in this very tower. He is fortunate still to be alive but I would not fancy his chances too highly in the future. But, princess, since you mentioned the council, I must tell you it has not been idle. It met on the eve of the prince's departure to discuss the question of the succession. The Earl of Tuscade reported, and I have to admit his remarks had the ring of truth to them, that you told him you love no man. That your only love is for Voravia. The council found this most commendable, but we have to be practical. As your closest relative is the prince, he has been declared your heir and that, in the event of your untimely death, he would be king. I need hardly add that given the deplorable state of the earl's health, it is only a matter of time before the Lady Barbara succeeds the prince.' Sir Ferdinand shifted in his chair and gave Lucy a slow smile.

'Ridiculous! It is true I told the earl I loved no man, but that is not to say I will not love one in the future. I am only fifteen.'

'Oh I know that. But what could I do? The others would have outvoted me. Anyway it's academic. For, princess, you will not have the chance to find this man. You will, this evening, fall from that window as you attempt to escape and in the morning your poor broken body will be found in the dried moat, your pretty neck snapped like Vladimar's. Come to think of it, your dress as a boy, and in disguise, will only add verisimilitude to the story.'

Again Lucy felt faint. She clutched at the windowsill for support. The room spun. Her heart was pounding. She bit her lower lip. She would not cry. She took five or six deep breaths.

She clenched her teeth and said slowly to herself, 'I am the last of a long and valiant line, the only hope of my people. I will not wilt as my enemies expect me to because I am a woman. I have an education the equal of any man. If I am to die I will be as brave as the Duke of Flanders. But before I die, I will think.'

Lucy went over to her desk, sat down and took her missal from the bookcase. She opened it and bent her head as if to study.

'What are you doing?' Ferdinand came across and looked over her shoulder, she caught the rank smell of wine on his breath.

'Lot of superstition, in my opinion.'

He returned to his seat.

Lucy turned to her miserable maid. 'Elspeth, let us have some light and also please close the shutters, the night is cool.'

As soon as Lucy had a candle she returned to her contemplation. She recalled William Salt's advice, 'Look at the world around you with fresh eyes and an open mind. There is some use in everything. Many times it is possible to adapt something to our advantage.' Lucy lifted her head and let her eyes roam slowly around the room. She was searching for a new use to every item. Her glance fell on Ferdinand. His eyes were closed. He was dozing.

How much had he had to drink? She wondered.

Then she saw something. Her heart gave a jump. Could it be she had the solution to the principal problem? It was possible. Of course, even if it were, there were other difficulties to overcome. She bent her head over her book and set her mind to thinking. Gradually a plan began to form in her mind. She determined to think it through in complete detail. What had William Salt said? 'The answer you first hit upon is not necessarily the right one. Put it aside in your mind and rethink the problem.'

The first necessity was to explain everything to Elspeth. She must persuade Ferdinand to leave the room, if only for a few minutes. He had been drinking. Perhaps she could exploit this weakness. But first she would need to forewarn Elspeth so that, as soon as Ferdinand left, she would be ready for her part.

How could she alert Elspeth, who was almost broken by fear?

Lucy rose. Ferdinand was awake in an instant. Lucy walked across to her prie-dieu.

'Elspeth, you and I must prepare ourselves. Come over and kneel beside me. You may bring your pillow to protect your knees.'

'I can't, my lady. I can't think of nothing to say.'

'There you are, princess, when she most needs your faith she loses it,' sneered Ferdinand.

'Elspeth, you will do me a great service by kneeling beside me. Go and get your pillow.' Lucy adopted as calm but authoritative a tone as she could.

Elspeth went to her room and returned with her pillow. She passed it to Lucy who placed it beside her prie-dieu. Lucy knelt down and motioned to Elspeth to do the same. Elspeth sank to her knees. Lucy placed her elbows on the ledge.

'Sit up. Clasp your hands as you should,' she commanded.

Elspeth did so and her head was now close to Lucy's.

'Mistress I must use my pot, I'm bursting.'

'It's nerves.' Lucy retorted. She was terrified Tuscade would arrive before she had managed to explain matters to Elspeth. It was only this little delay that gave them any hope of escaping death.

Elspeth turned a face contorted with misery.

'Oh all right,' Lucy replied. Then a thought struck her, 'Elspeth you are to piss in your water bucket,' she whispered. 'No don't argue. Then come back here.'

When Elspeth returned, Lucy motioned to her to take her place beside her.

'Now say quietly with me the Lord's Prayer.'

The girls recited the prayer, Lucy ensuring the words were said slowly and as reverently as she could.

'Elspeth,' Lucy whispered in the same manner as she would a prayer, 'I am going to tell you something. You must show no surprise.' There was a pause. 'Whisper back to me that you will stay completely calm.'

'Yes, my lady.'

'First I will say another prayer. It's for my plan. Dear God, grant that we, your children, may succeed in our endeavour. Amen.'

'Amen.' Elspeth's response was heartfelt.

'Elspeth, I'm going to try to get Ferdinand to

leave for a few minutes. Once he has gone, I will explain what we must do and your part. You must not argue. You must do exactly as I tell you. I think we have a chance of escaping. Whisper to me that you understand.'

'I will, my lady. You know I will.'

Elspeth looked at Lucy and her eyes were wide and shining with hope.

'I will say one last prayer. It will be a solemn one to ask forgiveness for our sins and to pray for life eternal should we fail.'

Lucy said her prayer and both girls said 'amen' together.

Lucy rose. She felt strangely calm, almost happy. Whether it was due to her devotions or the formulation of her plan, she did not know.

'We are ready, Sir Ferdinand. Now I would very much like a draught of wine. Have you any about you?'

This was the moment. Would he leave or shout to a servant?

Chapter 27

THE PLAN

Ferdinand looked astonished. He paused. Lucy guessed that it was exactly what he too would like. It would give him the courage to carry out his dreadful mission.

'I've none with me, but I'll fetch some.'

'I would be pleased if it were a good wine, Sir Ferdinand, not the very inferior kind Vladimar occasionally supplied me with.' Ferdinand would have to go to the palace cellars. Lucy hoped this would give her more time.

'It will be. I assure you.'

Ferdinand rose hurriedly. He left the room, locking the door behind him.

As soon as Ferdinand had had time to start his descent, Lucy handed Elspeth the heavy bible, opened her chest and took out one of Elspeth's linen skirts. Then she took a candle and her water bucket and led the way down the passage to the maid's room. She placed the light on the wash handstand, tipped the water from her bucket into Elspeth's. Even with her maid's recent contribution it was still barely three- quarters full. She hoped it would be sufficient for the task.

She turned to Elspeth. 'Elspeth, you need to be able to barricade your door. We'll knock out one of the pegs from your bed and, once I've left, you must jam it in the gap between the door and its frame. It needs to stop the door opening but not to resist a really hard thrust.'

Lucy explained the rest of her plan, pausing at intervals to enquire if Elspeth understood.

'And you can hide it under here.' She finished by indicating the skirt on the chair by the door.

When she had finished she asked Elspeth if she had any questions. Elspeth asked about two matters of detail and then Lucy told Elspeth to repeat back to her what she was to do. When she was satisfied, Lucy placed the Bible on the floor and lifted Elspeth's bed up so that one of the pegs rested upon the thick book. Then both girls sat down as heavily as they could on the side of the bed. The peg slipped out.

'Now for the bed,' said Lucy, 'will you be able to manage?'

'Yes, my lady.'

Lucy leant forward and kissed Elspeth lightly on her perspiring forehead. 'We'll win, you see. Now jam the door behind me'

Lucy stepped outside, turned and took the key from the door. She was about to drop it into the pocket in her breeches, when a thought struck her. She decided to check the ease of slipping it back into the lock in the gloom and turning it. For a second, panic seized her. It would not turn. She pulled the door hard towards her with the latch. The key turned. After pausing to collect herself, she unlocked the door and heard Elspeth shove the peg home. She tested the door with a push. It did not open. Then she returned to her room and sat herself demurely at her desk with her missal opened before her, the feel of the heavy key on her thigh a constant reminder of their plan.

Twenty minutes passed and still Ferdinand had not returned. Elspeth removed the peg and cautiously opened the door to her room.

'Princess, everything's ready. I've closed the shutter. With no candle it'll be pitch black. Shall we start on your bed?'

Lucy thought. She had expected Ferdinand long before now. But would they have time to do everything before he came back? Probably not. She would stick to her original plan. It was their best hope.

'No, we'll wait another hour. I'll set my sand timer. If he's not back by then we'll assume he's not coming. Go back, but keep your door just ajar. When you see him enter, close it quietly and jam it. Then wait for my call.'

Ten more minutes passed and then Lucy saw a light below the outer door and heard Ferdinand push the key into the lock and turn it. She gave a silent prayer of thanks that she had refused the temptation to start her escape and added, as an afterthought, one that hoped Elspeth had shut and wedged her door.

Sir Ferdinand swung the door open and entered, holding a lantern in one hand and the pitcher of wine in the other.

'Look who I have here,' he said gesticulating to the man who followed him.

Lucy felt a jolt of panic. Her plan had not envisaged having to deal with two enemies. She had hoped they would have escaped long before Tuscade's arrival. The only consoling thought was his appearance. Even in the poor light cast by the lantern, he looked dreadful. His skin was waxy white and wet with sweat. His lips were parted and a bubble of foam laced them. His dark hair had an oily tinge to it. He was shivering and panting from the exertion of the climb. His attire was dishevelled. In his hand he carried a short whip. He stood, swaying in the doorway with one hand on the doorpost, then lurched past Ferdinand to the oak armchair and collapsed into it. Perhaps he would not pose too much of a threat.

Le Gray locked the door and dropped the key into the inside pocket of his doublet. He carried the wine to the table and set it down.

Lucy called out, 'Elspeth, bring me three tankards.'

There was no reply.

'Where's your maid?' Ferdinand asked.

'She went to her room. She's terrified.'

'I really don't think she has much to fear from him tonight. This raises a small problem. For I had felt, princess, it would be fitting if your last memory would be of the humiliation and pain your maid suffered at the hands of my future brother. But I doubt he has the energy to perform the task, delightful though it was to be, that he had set himself for this evening. So I have come up with a solution. I shall act in Tuscade's place.'

The Earl of Tuscade tried to respond, but only managed a perfunctory snort. Ferdinand removed the whip from Tuscade's hand and began to loosen his jerkin.

Chapter 28

BREECHES

'Elspeth, Elspeth come here,' Lucy shouted out the signal she had arranged for Elspeth to use her candle.

There was a pause. 'Help! Help! Oh help!' Elspeth's cries reached them.

Before either man could move, Lucy darted down the passageway to Elspeth's door. She lifted the latch and pushed. It moved a fraction then jammed.

'It's stuck,' she called back, 'there's a fire in there, quick.'

Ferdinand was at her shoulder. He was carrying the lantern. Lucy had not thought of that.

'Break it down, Sir Ferdinand. Here, give me the lantern. I'll hold the latch.'

Ferdinand passed the lantern to Lucy who held it up. They could smell the smoke and hear the flames.

Ferdinand threw himself at the door. It burst open. He staggered into the smoke-filled room. A fire was blazing over in the corner as the dry straw from Elspeth's mattress took hold. In front of the fire Elspeth stood, holding her pail of water, as if frozen in fear.

Lucy put the lantern down and pushed the key into the keyhole.

She saw Ferdinand recover his balance and take three rapid strides towards Elspeth.

'Give me that, you stupid idiot.' He snatched the

pail from Elspeth, who slipped behind him as he threw the contents at the flames.

Immediately the room was plunged into darkness as the flames died.

As Lucy felt Elspeth step past her with the rope from her truckle bed, she pulled the door shut. She heaved on the latch and felt the key turn. Then she took it out and dropped it into the pocket of her breeches. She doused the lantern.

Lucy paused to listen.

There was a crash, as Ferdinand fell over the bed, followed by an oath. Then he was at the door scrabbling for the latch.

'Tuscade, help me! They've locked me in.'

There was no reply.

Lucy and Elspeth crouched in the dark of the passage.

Just behind them they heard Ferdinand, now frantic, roar, 'Tuscade, for God's sake, get me out.'

The Earl of Tuscade rose shakily and turned towards the passageway. As it was in total darkness Lucy knew he could see neither her nor Elspeth. But she could make out Tuscade's shambolic figure, outlined by the light from the candle.

'Take the key,' she whispered to Elspeth and passed it over.

Lucy crept down the corridor. When she was a few feet from the earl, she took a deep breath, rocked slightly back on her heels and hurled herself at the earl. Her head caught him just below the ribcage and completely by surprise. He reeled back, his thigh hit the arm of the chair and he crashed backwards over it, his hands flew up and his head smashed into something hard.

Lucy picked herself up as Elspeth came into the room and looked down at the motionless figure.

'Is he dead?'

Lucy bent down and put her ear to Tuscade's mouth. She could hear a bubbling sound.

'No, but I think he's unconscious. If he stirs hit him with the key. Now for the bed.'

Elspeth collected the candle and set it on the floor. Then she went over to the earl, lifted his doublet and undid the clasp on his belt. She heaved it free from the loops on Tuscade's breeches.

'We can tie his hands with this, my lady. Can you help me roll him over?'

'Yes, that's an excellent idea. Well done, Elspeth.'

They rolled the comatose earl over, dragged his hands behind his back and Elspeth wound the belt round the wrists. She pulled it so tight that they saw the flesh bulge beneath the thong. Elspeth fixed the buckle. Lucy put the key in her pocket.

Suddenly Elspeth seized the earl's breeches and pulled them down until they were round his ankles. A bloodstained bandage swathed the ulcer on his right calf.

'He'll not be able to get far like that.' She laughed.

Le Gray was pounding at the door and shouting to Tuscade.

When he paused Elspeth shouted back, 'Save your breath, he's dead to the world.'

There was a pause, then le Gray's tone altered.

'Of course I was never going to harm you, princess. It was just a joke. If you let me out I'll use all my influence to have you set free. I promise that. With my help you won't need to marry Tuscade. Now please let me out. We can be allies.'

'Oh shut up, you lying reptile.' Elspeth was in high good humour.

Lucy had thrown the mattress off her bed and was working at the first knot.

'This is very hard,' she muttered.

The next moment Elspeth was by her side with Tuscade's dagger. She hacked her way through the rope by the knot and repeated the treatment to the other end.

It took a matter of seconds to unlace the rope from the slots in the frame.

Lucy picked up an end of each rope and was about to tie them together when Elspeth grabbed Lucy's mattress and tipped the straw from it.

'We could use this cover as well. It will make the rope a bit longer,' she said.

'Yes, let's.' Lucy set about tying the cover to one rope then she added the second rope to the other end of the cover.

Taking one side of each knot in both hands she told Elspeth to take the other.

'Pull, Elspeth, our lives are going to depend on these knots.'

They held.

Lucy went over to the prie-dieu and started to drag it across the floor. She looked up to ask Elspeth to help and saw that her maid was standing over the prone body of Tuscade. She had Tuscade's knife in her hand.

'What are you doing? Come over here and help me shift this.'

'Shall I neuter him? He'll never trouble no women again. I know how to. I've seen my father geld a horse. It'll only take a moment.'

Lucy paused for a second. She was tempted to allow Elspeth to do so.

'No, Elspeth, there has been enough summary justice of late. When I'm queen he'll be given a fair trial. Now give me the knife and then help me.'

Elspeth joined her and they lugged the prie-dieu until its ledge was directly below the windowsill. Lucy opened the shutters. It was a fine night with a high wind. Moonlight flooded into the room. The full moon appeared to be racing across the sky. One moment it rode clear, the next, it had darted behind a cloud.

Lucy climbed up on the prie-dieu taking an end of the rope.

The moon reappeared and she looked down. The castle wall fell away below her in an enormous drop. In the moonlight she seemed to be even higher than by day. At the foot of the wall, the ground dropped steeply into the old moat. But there should be plenty of footholds in the gaps between the ancient weather-worn stones. She just hoped Elspeth had a head for heights like hers and not Peter Salt's.

She tied the rope to the central vertical bar.

'Pull with all your might.'

Elspeth seized the rope and heaved on it.

Lucy examined the knot. It had tightened but seemed sound.

'I'm going to throw it out. Then I'll climb down a short way. The wall's quite rough. We should be able to put our feet on it and walk down holding the rope.'

She gathered the rope up from Elspeth and dropped it down. She peered down. In the moonlight she could see the end swinging gently. It did not reach the bottom. They would have to jump and then roll down the grass into the old moat.

'Pass up the knife, Elspeth. We don't want there to be any chance they'll cut the rope.' She tossed it out of the window.

Chapter 29

A MIDDEN

'Are you ready, Elspeth?' Lucy asked

'Yes, my lady.'

Lucy knelt on the sill, facing into the room. She took a firm hold on the bar to the window and slid her legs out, then she eased herself between two of the bars until her pelvis rested on the edge. She let go with her left hand and felt down until she could grasp the rope. She lowered herself down until her right arm was at full stretch. Gripping with her feet she released her right hand and grabbed the rope.

Lucy paused. She was clear of her cell.

She swung her feet onto the wall and found the top of a stone. Pressing down, the weight came off her hands. She was standing on the wall, her hands on the rope merely preventing her from falling outwards. The moon emerged from a cloud and Lucy felt herself as exposed as if she were in full daylight. Her heart, already racing, missed a beat. There was no going back.

'I'm ready for you, Elspeth. Climb onto the sill. Lower your legs onto my shoulders.'

Lucy saw Elspeth's head appear in the frame of the window. One glance and it drew back.

'I can't. I'm scared. Oh, it's too high for me. Oh mistress, I'll never do it.'

Lucy looked up. 'You're as bad as Peter Salt. Elspeth, you remember I told you about the handsome young man who fought as your champion? Well, his name is Peter Salt and the man he fought and beat was Ferdinand le Gray. We'll go to Peter's home tonight.'

Elspeth's head reappeared. 'Peter Salt! He's gorgeous. I always thought he was the one you secretly loved and I was sure he loves you.'

'Now come on, Elspeth. If you want to meet him again you must come down here. Turn round, lie on your belly and lower your legs. I will guide them on to my shoulders. You'll be alright. Just don't look down. Hurry!'

Elspeth swivelled round and gingerly slid down onto her stomach. Very slowly she squeezed her way out until her legs hung down.

Lucy took the left one gently and placed it on her left shoulder.

'Push down on my shoulder Elspeth, and grip the bar with one hand.

Lucy felt Elspeth's weight and took her right leg and put that on her other shoulder.

'Stand up on me.' Lucy braced her legs on the rough wall. 'I'm going to move down a little. Lower yourself down as I do so.'

Lucy searched with her left leg for the next foothold, found it and placing one hand on Elspeth's foot lowered herself down, pulling Elspeth with her.

'Reach down with one hand for the rope.' Lucy saw Elspeth's hand appear and find the rope.

'Well done, Elspeth. Now transfer your other hand to the rope.' Lucy's legs and arms were aching from the effort of supporting Elspeth.

‘I’m going to put one of your feet on the wall. Don’t worry you will find it easy.’

She took hold of Elspeth’s right foot and placed it in a crack in the wall.

‘There, now the other one.’

Lucy heaved a sigh of relief as she saw Elspeth now had both feet on the wall.

‘Now follow me slowly down. Grope with one foot for a hold and then move the second one down.’

The moon disappeared. She restrained the urge to go down as quickly as she knew she could. After three or four movements Elspeth’s confidence grew and they began to make good progress. They passed the floor beneath theirs and then the next one. Shortly below this Lucy came to the knot that joined the first of the ropes to her mattress cover. A fear seized her. Would the hessian hold their weight? Gingerly she moved her hands down onto it, she felt a slight give in the material, but it seemed strong enough. Soon she was onto the second rope and now her fear was re-doubled. The hessian would have to bear both their weights. She cursed herself for not arranging the rope so that the cover was at the bottom end. She tried desperately to ensure all her weight was on the stonework. She edged slowly down. Elspeth was on the second rope by now. The cover seemed to be holding. They passed two more floors and then suddenly Lucy was at the end of the rope.

‘In a moment I’m going to jump. When you get here, turn round. Face away from the wall and leap. As soon as you touch the ground fall forward, roll yourself into a ball and you'll somersault down the hill. Do you understand, Elspeth?'

'Yes, yes, I'll be fine.'

Lucy turned herself round, took a deep breath and jumped. She hit the ground. Instead of her plan of falling forward and rolling down the hill her heels slipped on the dew-covered turf and she slid down the bank and arrived in a heap at the bottom. As Lucy got to her feet, Elspeth arrived, cannoning into Lucy and the two of them collapsed into a stinking swamp.

'Where are we?' asked Elspeth.

'By the smell, in a midden.' replied Lucy.

They climbed to their feet. Suddenly Elspeth burst out laughing and threw her arms round Lucy.

'Oh, Lucy, you done it, you done it!'

'No, Elspeth. We done it. You were quite wonderful. But what a stink!'

Lucy was crying and laughing at the same time.

They stood there hugging each other and sobbing with laughter.

Eventually, Lucy pulled herself free. 'Let's get going. We must find your handsome admirer.'

Lucy took Elspeth's hand and the two of them began to squelch their way, calf deep, through the filthy cesspit, stumbling their way through nettles and rushes. They reached the far side and started to climb the bank. A little way up they crossed the track that Lucy recognised as the way from the stable yard to the gallops. She paused to consider following it up but realised it would only lead them to the locked gate into the stables. She found a small path that climbed the bank with walls on either side.

Suddenly a dog some way ahead of them began to bark furiously. Other hounds took up the chorus.

Lucy paused. 'Come on, they'll only start again next time we move.'

They reached the top of the bank as the moon came out from behind a cloud. Ahead of them was a narrow lane that led between two houses. The dog was tethered at the back door of the one to their left. A window opened and a voice shouted, 'Shut up.'

It made no difference it was wild with excitement.

Lucy and Elspeth hurried past. They reached a street. Lucy looked about. Then, glancing up, she saw the huge bulk of the tower of St. Stephano's silhouetted against the stars.

'We'll make for the cathedral, this way.'

They crept along, hugging the walls of the houses. Suddenly a window opened a voice called out 'gardez l'eau' and emptied the contents of a chamber pot on Elspeth's head.

Elspeth jumped in surprise.

Lucy could not help giggling and whispered, 'Do you know, I think you smell a bit better now.'

They reached a thoroughfare at right angles. The houses immediately in front of them now hid the tower. Lucy turned to the left, resolving to take the next street on the right. When they came to it she saw the side of the cathedral, now close at hand. They slunk forward until they reached the open space that surrounded the great church.

Lucy had no idea which way to turn. She looked up at the stars, picked up the seven stars of the Plough and located the pole star. Once again she silently thanked William Salt for his lessons. Facing the star, west must be to her left.

'This way, Elspeth. When we get to the front of the Cathedral. I'll know where I am.'

In front of the west door of the Cathedral was the open square where the market was held. It was bathed in moonlight like a stage set. The houses on the far side were in deep shadow. Whitefriars, the street with the Salts' shop in it, was somewhere over there. They would have to cross the square. The moon slipped behind a cloud.

'Now.' Lucy took Elspeth by the hand and they began to lope across the open space.

They saw a light approaching down one of the streets in front of them. It was the watchman.

'Quick, back into the porch,' Lucy hissed to Elspeth.

They made the porch before the watchman entered the square. They flattened themselves against the wall. The watchman paused, then turned to his left and walked along the far side and entered another street.

'Now. Run, but quietly'

They reached the far side of the square and paused for breath. The houses here were more substantial.

Lucy racked her brain to try to recall which of the streets was the right one. Then she recognised a cobbler's sign. This must be it.

As they started down the roadway a cat raced across in front of them. Both girls jumped in alarm.

'The shop's on the right,' Lucy whispered.

They slipped along in the shadows. The shops were shuttered and all looked much the same. Then they were there. Lucy had been to it so many times in the old days, she instantly knew it.

Lucy went up to the door and beat on it with her fist. Nothing happened. Elspeth joined her. Still there was no response. An appalling thought struck her. Was no one in?

Chapter 30

BROTH

Lucy remembered the key. She reached into her pocket, took it out and hammered on the door. A window flew open above them and Abigail's tousled head appeared.

'What do you want? It's the middle of the night.'

'It's me. Lucy. Princess Lucia. Please let us in. We're in great danger.'

'William, wake up. It's the princess. Quick open the door.'

At that moment Lucy heard the watchman at the far end of the street. He was walking slowly towards them. The girls pressed themselves into the doorway. Then, when the man was only thirty paces away, the bolts were pulled aside. The door opened and Lucy and Elspeth fell into the astonished arms of William Salt.

The door closed seconds before the watchman came up to it. He passed by.

Abigail appeared at the foot of the stairs and then Peter.

'I'm afraid we smell most dreadfully, Abigail. I'm sorry to bring our stink into your clean home.'

Lucy's reserve left her. She burst into tears. She stood there sobbing, her chest heaving with the effort. Abigail threw her arms round her. She stroked her hair as she had Peter's when he was a little child.

'Come into the kitchen. I'll find some honey and we will make you both an infusion.'

William Salt took Elspeth's hand, but Elspeth was by now also in tears, her hands to her eyes. Peter took hold of her and ran his fingers through her hair.

'Ugh, Elspeth, what have you got in your hair? It feels like, oh it can't be.'

Now Elspeth's tears turned to laughter. 'Oh it is. Someone tipped their pot all over me.'

Then she raised her muck-smeared face and kissed Peter full on the lips. It was a very inexperienced sort of kiss. Rather wet, but full of enthusiasm.

The next moment the whole company was in stitches.

Ten minutes later, Abigail had stripped both girls and was washing them with some warm water from the copper. William was heating the honey, wine and water and Peter was studiously watching his father so that both men had their backs to the girls.

'You can turn round now,' said Abigail, as she slipped the second nightgown over Elspeth.

Peter turned around. Lucy was wearing Abigail's best nightdress the one her father had given his daughter eighteen years ago - on the eve of her marriage to William. It was of cream silk. Elspeth's was of a rougher linen. In the soft candlelight he could make out the forms of their bodies beneath the folds of their nightdresses. Lucy had the athletic frame of a boy. Elspeth filled her nightdress deliciously with her soft feminine curves. She looked overcome with joy and happiness.

Peter held out a chair for Lucy and fetched a stool for Elspeth from the shop. She turned a radiant, heart-stopping smile to him. William poured a measure from the pan into the pottery mugs that Abigail had placed in front of them. Then the three Salts joined them round the table.

The girls took a sip of the delicious brew. Lucy felt her head spinning.

'Abigail, do you have any bread, I'm famished?'

'Oh, my children, of course you are. When did you last eat?'

'I think it was yesterday at noon.'

Abigail rose, then it dawned on her what she had said.

'Princess, I mean Queen Lucia, I'm sorry I addressed you in that way.' She paused then added softly, 'from daylight tomorrow you will not have a more loyal, respectful or humble subject than Abigail Salt. But, just for this one magical night, please allow me to treat you and your friend as though you were the two little girls I longed to have.'

'Oh yes, yes please do. Magical night. Yes, that is just what it is. What a beautiful phrase. Oh would that time could stand still.'

'Magical night,' repeated Peter, 'how strange, Henry Martley used that very phrase when he was telling me of a play he's writing.'

'Henry Martley, have you seen him lately?' Lucy enquired.

'No. I've missed him. We have become the best of friends,' said Peter

'Oh, he is mine too. I too miss him,' Lucy replied softly.

The way Lucy said these words would, under normal circumstances, have stabbed Peter to the heart. But the memory of Elspeth's kiss had quite changed matters. A kiss from Lucy, and it was something he had imagined hundreds of times during the war, would, he suspected, be rather a chaste affair. Nothing like the spontaneous and generous one he had just received from her maid. His mind was in a whirl. His affection for Lucy and the impossibility of anything coming of it had, he thought, been something he would have to suffer for the rest of his life. Now he was being subjected to a very different emotion. It was like the difference between the steady heat of a farrier's furnace and the blaze of a bonfire.

Abigail busied herself at the fire. 'You shall have some of Brother Simon's marrow broth, that's the most nourishing food there is.'

'Brother Simon, is he here?'

'Yes he is,' Peter replied, 'He's been here for three weeks. At first he was quite delirious but we now think he'll pull through. He was nearly killed in the same forest where your good father, the great king, was struck down. He can tell us nothing about what happened that terrible afternoon.'

Abigail brought the hot broth and a loaf of bread to the table, poured a generous helping into two wooden bowls and gave each girl a spoon. The candle threw a warm, friendly circle of light on the wooden table. Lucy drank her soup, ate her bread and sipped her drink. She closed her eyes and felt she had never been so happy and contented in all her life.

'Come on girls, you're falling asleep at the table. Into bed with you! You'll have William's and my bed, and please don't argue.'

She led the way up to the cosy bedroom and pulled back the coverlet. Then she took each girl in turn, gave them a hug and a goodnight kiss and left.

Lucy knelt down at the bed and Elspeth knelt beside her. Both girls thought back to the last time they had done this and of all the events that had followed.

'Say a prayer for both of us, my lady, you do it so well.'

Then they climbed into the still warm bed and lay there side by side.

'He is rather gorgeous, isn't he?' Lucy said in a dreamy voice.

'Oh, if you love him, he's yours. Don't worry about me,' Elspeth said quickly, if a little sadly.

'Oh no, no, I'm not his type at all. Handsome warriors, like Peter Salt, much prefer pretty, high-spirited girls like you.' Lucy was not sure whether she really meant this. 'Poor boy, I fear the sight of us two girls in our nightdresses really confused him. He may be able to handle a sword or a horse but put him in front of a half-naked girl or up a ship's masthead and he's as timid as a house mouse.'

There was a little pause then she added, 'By the way I shall need a new lady-in-waiting. I'm not having that dreadful Barbara. I can think of no one as loyal and pleasant to be with than my Elspeth. I should like you to take the position.'

‘Oh, my lady, I’m not good enough.’

‘Nonsense, Elspeth, you are the best lady in all the land and the bravest.’

Elspeth was about to protest when a change in Lucy’s breathing told her that she was beyond any more conversation.

Chapter 31

A TOW-HAIRED WITCH

Lucy woke with a start. For a second she could not think where she was. A small amount of the morning sunshine filtered in around the edges to the shuttered window and, in the low light, the room she was in seemed unusually small. Then there was the hubbub from the street outside. All her life her bedrooms had been large and quite luxurious, their surroundings hushed. Now she could hear shouts from traders and carriers so close they could have been in the room. Then the events of the previous night came flooding back to her. To her left Elspeth lay still asleep. A ray of sunshine glinted on the jumble of bronze curls strewn across the pillow. Lucy shook her newly appointed lady-in-waiting awake.

'Come on Elspeth, heaven knows what the time is. It sounds as if it must be midday already.'

The two girls climbed out of the bed and blearily made their way downstairs. They found a family conference in progress.

'My lady, how did you sleep?' Abigail jumped to her feet. Now that the magical night had passed she had, as promised, become a most loyal subject.

'Oh very well, thank you. I feel terrible to have taken your bed.'

The Salts moved away from the table to allow the two girls to breakfast. They ate in silence.

It was broken by a creak from the staircase. Lucy

looked up to see Brother Simon coming slowly down, clutching the handrail. He was very unkempt and in much need of a razor. But his eye was bright and his step, although tentative, steady. He was dressed in the black and white friar's robe that Abigail had laundered when he had first arrived.

'Brother, how are you feeling?' Peter asked.

'Much better, thank you. I don't know how to thank you all. You saved my life.' He paused then gasped, 'Princess, what are you doing here?'

William said, 'Brother Simon, you'll be wondering about many things and in due course Peter will be able to answer most of your questions but, for the moment, I'd ask you to restrain your curiosity whilst we hear the princess' s story.'

Brother Simon indicated his agreement.

'Now, princess, please can you tell us what danger you are in and then I hope we can help?'

The princess related the events since the dreadful news of her father's death. On occasions, one of her listeners would interrupt with a question.

'The Earl of Tuscade? asked Peter. 'I never met him.'

'You haven't missed anything,' responded Elspeth, 'he's the most horrible man. He was going to rape me and then all sorts of terrible things and in the end kill me. An' he would have done it if it had not been for the princess,' she added.

'If I ever get the chance he'll pay for that. By God he will,' snapped Peter.

'Well, he's very fortunate the princess was present

when I had him with his breeches down.' Elspeth laughed then added, 'Oops, sorry, Brother.'

When Lucy had finished her story and Elspeth had added all those parts that the princess had omitted in modesty, the Salts sat in stunned silence.

'So, you two young girls, with no weapons and nothing but your wits to fight with, overpowered two grown men, one a knight of the realm. You managed to imprison them, improvised a means of climbing down from a great height and found your way to this shop. Princess Lucia, you will make a wonderful queen,' said William. 'Any nation lucky enough to have so resourceful and brave a leader should think itself truly blessed.'

'I could never ever have done it without thinking like you taught me, William. If ever I do regain my throne, there will be a complete change in the teaching in our schools and universities.' Lucy nodded her head emphatically. Then she added, 'Oh, I nearly forgot. How could I? The last thing I did before falling asleep last night was to appoint Elspeth as my lady-in-waiting.'

'Congratulations, Elspeth,' said Peter. 'I hope, your ladyship, that your new status will not mean you will lose all your sense of fun.'

Elspeth rose, gave a rather awkward curtsy, and turned a laughing face to him, 'On the contrary, squire Peter, I shall have the more opportunities to indulge it. There, you see, I am quite the lady already.'

William bought the party back to the seriousness of their situation.

'The first priority is to find both of you some fresh clothes. You can't live in nightdresses and those clothes you arrived in are quite unsuitable. Then we need to get the pair of you out of Voravia as soon as we can. The first refuge for anyone in trouble in Voravia is Sloronia and I am sure King Francois and the Duke D'Urbin would be delighted to cause trouble for Voravia by shielding its rightful queen.'

'I shall not go to Sloronia. I'd rather die here than ally myself with our enemy.'

'I knew that would be your response, princess, and you are quite right. Even if the Sloronians succeeded in installing you on your throne you would be indebted to them forevermore. No, it will have to be England, but that means we need to find a ship. In the meantime we must find somewhere for you to hide. Nieuport is the most dangerous place. The prince and Ferdinand will be bound to start a search for you and the first place they will look is here. We must slip you out into the countryside as soon as possible. I'm wondering if that farmer who looked after Brother Simon would help us.'

'They will have to be in disguise. Elspeth doesn't pose too much of a problem. We can dye her hair and she will pass for one of any number of girls of her age,' said Abigail. 'The princess is more difficult. She will be recognised.'

'We must ask ourselves what her enemies would least expect her to wear. I think there are two possibilities. She could be dressed as a young man of noble birth or as a serving girl.' William said.

'Well, it'll certainly be easier to explain the presence of a servant than a visiting young noble, should we get a visit,' Peter said.

'And a visit we will get. This is one of the first places they'll look.' William said.

'Two servants in a little house like this is bound to raise their suspicions,' Abigail said.

'You are right Mistress Salt. We need some other explanation for two strangers. But what?' Brother Simon asked.

'That's it,' said Peter, 'we dress Lucy as a friar. Brother Simon, how do we get a robe like yours?'

'Oh, that's no problem. We just buy the material and make one,' Brother Simon replied.

'Abigail, you and Brother Simon must go to the market now and buy some cheap clothes for Elspeth and some material to make a habit for the princess. Peter and I will attend the shop, we do not want our behaviour to excite suspicion.' William said.

Within twenty minutes Abigail and Brother Simon returned with dire news.

'The first person we met told us the gates are closed. No one may leave without a thorough search of their person and their carts. The soldiers are searching every house, room by room and there are patrols in the streets. We heard one of the town criers telling everyone that the princess is nigh to death. It is from the fever she took three weeks ago when she walked in the hard weather at the funeral. They add that a tow-haired witch, purporting to be the Princess Lucia, is in hiding and that there is a reward of one hundred gold crowns for anyone who knows of her whereabouts.'

'Where are the soldiers now?' asked Peter.

'Close. In the next street. They'll be here within the half hour,' Abigail said.

There was a silence as everyone thought.

'If we hide the princess and she's found, that's the end. She must either be in the open or in so safe a place no one will think of looking for her,' said Peter.

'But where?' asked William.

There was a long pause as everyone tried to think of a safe place.

'I know,' Peter said. 'Where is the last place they'll look? Why, the castle. Right under their noses.'

'That's true. But how are we to get the princess there and, if we do, how do you think she'll eat?'

'Well, not perhaps exactly inside the walls but in the stables.' Peter turned to Lucy. 'I go twice a day to water and feed Belle and often I give her a ride. When I am at the stables I always look in on old Stang. He's very melancholy. He misses your good father as much as any of his loyal subjects. No one else goes near Stang so I've taken to attending to him as well as Belle. Stang's stable is well away from the other stalls and there's a tack room attached. It is not the most desirable of places to live. It is not suitable for a princess let alone a queen, but that's for the best. No one will think of looking there.'

'Oh, that would be perfect. I love old Stang,' said Lucy. 'He and I will be the best of friends. There is nobody I would rather share a home with.'

Peter felt a jolt in his heart at Lucy's words.

He swallowed, 'I think I must take Lucy, I mean the queen, there immediately. Brother Simon, did you buy any black serge?'

'No. We never got to the market.'

'She'll have to wear yours. It's but a short distance. With luck no one will notice its poor fit. Take it off, Brother, and give it to the princess quickly,' Peter said.

Brother Simon shot into the larder and a few seconds later the door opened and he passed out the Dominican habit.

Abigail draped it over the slim figure of Lucy. As Brother Simon had a slight frame, the fit was not too bad. With the girdle tied around her waist, the hood raised and clutching a bible she looked really most convincing.

Three minutes after the decision she and Peter stepped out of the door to the shop and turned towards the castle, as they left, Lucy heard Abigail turn her attention to Elspeth.

'Come on my girl. Let's get those pretty red curls of yours dyed black. William, we need some soot from the range.'

Chapter 32

STANG'S KISS

At the end of the street they saw four soldiers leave the first house.

'Follow me,' Peter whispered to Lucy and they crossed the narrow street towards the patrol.

'What's going on?' Peter asked the man in charge. 'Why it's Ben Watts, isn't it? How are you, sergeant?'

'Squire Peter, how are you? Haven't seen you since the battle in the snow. What a day! First the victory then the terrible death of King Charles, God bless him. Yes, Brother, may God have mercy on the good man.' The soldier crossed himself and nodded to Peter's companion. 'Well, I mustn't stay here gossiping. Got to search every damn house in this street by midday or there'll be trouble. Supposed to be looking for some young witch. Hardly soldiers' work really. I suppose you'll be looking for employ in some war or other. Everyone reckons you'll become a freelance in spite of my opinion of them villains.'

Peter clapped the man on the shoulder then turned to Lucy. 'Come on, Brother, I'll show you the palfrey your abbot was interested in.'

They walked on, trying not to hurry. They entered a small square. They were in the most ancient part of the town. On one side the houses huddled up against the great walls of the castle. The little ancient Church of St. Lazarus was squeezed into the far corner. The other side was composed of fine buildings in warm sandstone, originally the homes of merchants. There was a wellhead in the centre of the square and dotted around its edge some old lime trees, whose buds were just starting to show pale green. In the spring sunlight there was a delightful calm to the place.

A short alleyway led to the Royal stables. Peter strolled across the yard, either throwing cheery remarks to the stablemen and grooms or making suitable comments to the friar. Half way across the yard, Peter turned into a long building with several stalls, walked a short way down it until they came to Belle. The mare gave a whinny of delight and Peter found her a bucket of oats, all the while talking about the imagined horse the friar had come to see.

After what Peter judged to be a realistic time with Belle he led the way out into the yard.

I must show you my other friend. He's quite old now but there can be few finer horses in all Voravia.'

They turned into the passage that led to Stang's stable. At the end of it, Peter opened the door. A delightful smell of hay, horse and leather filled Lucy's nostrils. In the gloom she could make out the huge bulk of Stang. He shifted his weight and turned his head to look at the two young visitors. There was something so calm, so brave, so generous and so kind about Stang's great head with his huge soft eyes that Lucy knew he would protect her with his very life. She had known this great horse since her childhood.

Stang's stable was quite gloomy, lit as it was only by the half stable door and the tiny window set high in the opposite wall above his hay-rack.

Peter rummaged around in the straw in a corner and produced an ancient key. He pushed it into the lock of a door in one side of the stable, turned it and opened the door to a small tack room. He stood aside to allow Lucy to enter.

The door they had opened was in a wall that was only a partition. Both stable and tack room shared the same roof space. There was a wooden rack down the length of this wall and projecting from it a line of spigots over which were draped different saddles and pieces of horse armour. A series of hooks along the opposite wall held bridles, stirrups, girth straps and other harness accoutrements. The short far wall contained an old wooden door.

Lucy went across and tried to open it. It was locked.

'Do you know where that goes?' Peter enquired.

'It leads onto a little narrow alley that runs between the castle wall and the back of the stables. My father always referred to it as the snicket. Towards its end there's an old sally port in the castle walls. Few people know of it. I believe my father would come out that way when he wanted to visit the city incognito. I expect he used it when he called on your family all those years ago.'

'Do you know where the snicket comes out?'

'In that little square. Right up in one corner beside the old church. There's a sort of gate. It's probably locked but the key is in a recess in the castle wall. At least that's where I last saw it, ages ago.'

They resumed their examination of the room. There was a small barrel containing an assortment of metal work, spurs, bits and spare clips for attaching armour. Along the wall, beneath the small window, was a rough bench with the remnants of leather repairs strewn across it. Peter tipped the contents of the barrel into a corner, set it on its side and placed a light saddle on it.

'I'm afraid that's the best I can do for a seat. Now where can you sleep?'

They looked around. There seemed nowhere.

'In his manger. What was good enough for the King of Heaven is certainly good enough for the Queen of Voravia. I'll be well hidden there and Stang can keep an eye on me. Peter, when you next come, and come at your usual time, could you bring me some quills, ink and paper? I need something to occupy my time, apart from grooming Stang. Now you must go about your usual routine, attend to Belle, muck out her stable and then you can come back here and deal with Stang. That way no one will think you are behaving differently.'

When Peter had gone, Lucy spent a few minutes with Stang. In spite of his enormous size he instilled no fear in her. After putting her face against his lovely soft nose for a few seconds she returned to the tack room.

She sat herself at her makeshift desk and let the sunlight warm her arms. She was tempted to tidy the room to make it more like a home but then reasoned that she should do nothing to indicate someone was living there.

It was almost an hour before Peter returned and began to change Stang's straw. It was a hot day but Lucy suspected that was not the only reason he worked bare-chested. Standing in the gloom of the tack room, Lucy watched. The warm scent of horse and leather were heavy on the sultry air. The stable was dim but a beam of sunlight from the little high window illuminated tiny motes of dust that danced in the air. It also played on Peter's chest and arms. There was something dangerously attractive about the ripple of his muscles and the fine beads of perspiration on his skin. She found her breath was coming in quick, short gasps. It was both worrying and deliciously exciting. She felt light-headed, almost as if she were going to faint. During her captivity in the Dark Tower, the education had not all been one way. Lucy had taught Elspeth to read and, in return, her maid had told Lucy something of those most mysterious creatures - boys. Lucy had been surprised at Elspeth's enthusiasm for the male physique. Now she was beginning to understand it.

When Peter had finished he turned to Lucy. 'I really don't want to leave. I'm terrified you'll be found.'

Lucy returned to the real world from her reverie with a start. She took Peter's hand, lifted it and brushed it, light as a feather, with her lips and gave him her grave smile.

'Please don't worry, Peter. I'll be fine. Now off with you!'

Lucy watched Peter step out into the bright sunlight. She saw him look at his hand and raise it to his lips.

Lucy spent a long day attending to Stang. The solitude allowed her to dwell on an idea she had often turned over in her mind whilst a prisoner in the Dark Tower. Six months ago her father had passed her a book entitled *The Prince*. It was by an Italian economist called Niccolò Machiavelli. She had read it with some difficulty. It had not only been the technical nature of the writer's arguments, but her distaste for his ruthlessness. But his central premise that the new way of thinking applied as much to politics and government as to science, research and the arts was surely right. She would write her own thoughts on the subject, one in which her moral code would soften the Italian's, and in doing so have a plan for her reign. By the time the afternoon sun had started to flood through the window of the tack room, she felt that, not only had the great warhorse developed a real affection for her, but that she had a task to occupy her whilst she awaited the boat to England.

That evening Peter brought her some clothes, a supper of warm ham, fresh bread and stored apples, her quills and paper and desperate news.

'The town crier was out again this evening telling of your death and that your body would be taken to Voravine tomorrow for burial. The crier ended his announcement with the cry "Long live King Rupert". The rumour is that the coronation will take place next week.'

Peter was silent for a moment then he blurted out, 'Lucy, when the people heard the crier say you were dead, they were weeping in the streets. The prince and his men are hated. Everyone loves you,' Peter paused, then said very deliberately, 'and so do I.'

'I did rather hope you might. But Peter,' Lucy replied, 'the first priority is to rid Voravia of these wicked people. My subjects should not have to submit to the arbitrary rule of these evil men.'

The words came easily to her. She barely noticed they were those, not of a schoolgirl or a friend, but of a ruler.

'You are right, my lady, that is the only really important thing. What do you want from me? I promised your father, on his deathbed, I would serve you always.'

'Well the first thing, my loyal Sir Peter, is that you shall continue to call me Lucy.' She was already starting to regret the way she had spoken. She guessed he had been summoning up his courage for his declaration and she had snubbed him cruelly.

After Peter left to attend to Belle, Lucy changed into the simple shift Abigail had found. She would return Brother Simon's robe, when Peter next came. Then she ate her meal and drank some of Stang's water. As she did so she thought about what Peter had said. He was, she was sure, ready to die for her. Just like dear Flanders had been. Indeed the two of them had more in common than she had realised when she had teased him all those months ago. She gave a little sigh. His devotion was, like the duke's, rather spaniel-like. Were all decent men like that or only soldiers? No, with Elspeth he was at ease, laughing and joking. Was it her personality or her position that seemed to inspire a reserve in them? Well, it was probably a little of both. She found it difficult to imagine being able to kiss a boy in the same carefree way Elspeth had. But that did not stop her wondering what it felt like to be part of that sort of kiss. Her mind drifted back to her feelings when Peter had been working in the stable. They had not been those of love. She was sure she would recognise that fine emotion. No, it had been something much more primitive - desire. This was followed by a sad thought; perhaps queens and princesses could never behave in Elspeth's happy, uninhibited manner.

Lucy clenched her jaw. Her duty was to her nation. She laid out a sheet of paper, her quills and the jar of ink on the bench, arranged the makeshift seat in front of it and, in the late evening light that streamed in through the cobwebs in the window, wrote the title: *The rights and duties of monarch and subject in a free nation*. After an hour of concentrated thought and writing, the fading light forced her to stop. As night fell, she climbed into Stang's manger and curled up in his hay. The old warhorse bent his great head over Lucy's and she felt the slow, warm exhalation of his breath as he kissed her goodnight.

Chapter 33

THE SNICKET

The next morning Lucy decided to examine the door into the snicket. The lock closely resembled the one in the door between tack room and stable and, when she looked at this, it was obvious that it was a very crude affair. The tenon was of iron, but the mortice into which it fitted was a simple slot in the wood of the doorframe. The wood had hardened with time but Lucy reckoned that, with a chisel, it should be possible to cut enough of it to allow the door to open without turning the key.

She looked around the bench and quickly found a rather blunt chisel. A few minutes working the steel against first a rough stone in the wall and then one worn smooth by Stang's rubbing, produce a sharp edge.

She began to chisel away at the wood. It was old and very hard, but after an hour's work, she had made some progress. By the time Peter arrived with her breakfast, there was a small pile of wood shavings by the door.

'If we could open this door,' Lucy explained, 'you could come and go without having to dodge people in the yard.'

'Let me help.' Peter could see the obvious advantage this would give them.

'No, Peter, you must spend no more time here than you would normally. Besides it gives me something to pass the time.'

Lucy returned to her labour for another hour. Then tired, she put her chisel down and went over to the bench that was to be her writing table. She had barely started on her writing when Peter arrived with a pail of water for Stang. He was breathless.

'Quick, Lucy! Ferdinand's here with a search party. One of the men with him I recognise. He was with Ben Watts when we came in. I think he's told Ferdinand about my coming up here with the friar. They're searching the first row of stables now. I got in whilst they were all in there.'

Lucy felt her heart pound. It was likely Ferdinand would realize she was living in the tack room. They must hide all trace of her presence. She dragged open an old drawer in the bench. It was full of awls and other leather-working tools. She gathered up her papers, quills and ink and pushed them into the back, covered them with a saddle cloth and closed the drawer. She saw that Peter had turned the barrel over and was frantically filling it with the bits and stirrups. Suddenly she noticed the new wood revealed by her morning's work. It showed pale against the old weathered oak. She darted into Stang's stable and, with a grimace, scooped up some of his dung and worked it into the telltale scar. Then she bent down, cupped her hands round the shavings and threw them into Stang's straw.

Now where to hide? The tack room was so small and, although full of clutter, there was nowhere she could avoid being seen. She ran back into Stang's stable. Her first thought was the manger. Peter could cover her with straw. But Ferdinand would be bound to search there. Above the manger and high up was the tiny window.

Peter came through from the tack room.

'That window.'

Lucy pointed to it but, even as she did so, she knew it was almost certainly far too high and probably too small. Peter looked up at it for a brief moment, then put one foot on the water trough, a second on the manger and swung himself up onto the top bar of the hay-rack.

'Quick, Lucy. Up here,'

He knelt down, took Lucy's up-stretched hand and lifted her up. She steadied herself with one hand on the wall as Peter made a leap and managed to grab the main beam. He got a foot onto a protruding brick and within seconds he had hauled himself onto the beam dislodging a shower of dust and debris. Lying along its length, he reached down, took both of Lucy's hands and pulled her up.

The beam they were on ran the full width of both stable and tack room and was supported partway along its length by the dividing wall.

'You two search that line. You, soldier, come down here.' They heard Ferdinand shout an order. He would be in the stable any minute.

'Through there,' whispered Peter. 'Can you cross to the far wall? You should be safe there, unless Ferdinand looks up. Don't sneeze.'

Very carefully, with her left hand on the roof and

her right brushing aside the curtain of cobwebs that laced the roof space, she walked along the beam until she reached the far wall. She turned her back and leant against the wall and watched Peter as he swung himself down and dropped onto the straw in Stang's stable. She could look down directly below her into the tack room, which was lit by the window above the workbench.

She could hear, but not see, Peter as he began to muck out Stang.

'Why, Salt, I half expected to find you here.' Ferdinand was in the stable now and his voice had a trace of satisfied triumph to it.

'Good afternoon, Sir Ferdinand.' Peter's reply was polite. 'What brings you here?'

'I understand you brought a friar up to the stable yesterday. Is that true?'

'Yes, indeed it is.'

'I am told by this soldier that you left the yard alone.'

There was a slight pause then Peter replied. 'When I left the yard that man was not there. He could not have seen me. If that man says he saw me leave he is lying, hoping no doubt to get his hands on the reward. However, for the record, I did leave alone. I was here for an hour at least.'

'How did you come to be with that friar in the first place?'

'He came to our house.'

'Just as I thought. Then you brought her up here. Oh don't try to look surprised. I know she was that...

that witch who is telling folk she's the princess.'

'And why should some witch come to our house, Sir Ferdinand? It would seem a great coincidence.'

'Coincidence, rubbish! Of course she would come to your house. She studied there. It was the only place she knew.'

'Studied at our house? A country witch?' Peter gave a laugh. 'I think you're confusing her with the Princess Lucia. But the princess is ill, nigh to death, is she not, Sir Ferdinand?'

Lucy heard a sharp crack. 'Take that you insolent pup.'

She flinched as she imagined the blow to Peter.

'Stick a fork in that hay.' Ferdinand shouted, 'I'll take a look in here.'

She saw him enter the tack room. He looked about and then went over to the door. Lucy closed her eyes in fear. Would Ferdinand look up into the roof space? With horror she saw the dirt she had dislodged made a line across the floor. Ferdinand kicked some of it aside.

'Where does this door go?' he called out.

'Don't know, sir, 'tain't been opened for I don't know how long.' The head groom's voice came from outside.

Ferdinand took hold of the latch and pulled it. He stood looking around the room, then went over and began to feel behind a row of saddles hanging on pegs almost immediately beneath her.

'Nothing here, sir,' called the man from Stang's stable.

Ferdinand turned, he scratched his neck where some dust had landed and returned to the stable.'

'You told me you saw this man leave the stable yard, did you?' The menace in Ferdinand's voice reminded Lucy of his words in the tower.

'I…I, well I was suspicious, sir. I thought I should scare Squire Salt, like you asked us to.'

'You lied to me. No one lies to me and lives. You're under arrest.'

Lucy heard the men walk briskly down the alley. She slowly exhaled her breath. Ten minutes passed then Peter came into the tack room.

'They've left the yard. God knows what Ferdinand will do to that soldier. Ferdinand knew he'd let slip you were still alive. The chance that soldier would blab to his mates you hadn't died has sealed his fate. Jump down, I'll catch you.'

Lucy paused for a moment, dropped to her haunches and jumped. Peter caught her round the waist and lowered her to the ground. For just a few seconds they stood holding each other. The same strange sensation she had experienced when watching Peter swept through her but now it had a warmer feel to it. Part of it was the security a man's arms gave her, in the same way her father's had when he held her, but there was in addition the now familiar hint of danger and the unknown. Her heart was pounding. She felt a wild surge of excitement. They looked into each other's eyes and Peter gently wiped a cobweb from her brow. Then he relaxed his grip and stepped away. The moment had gone.

'I must be off. Ferdinand may be watching at the gates. If I stay too long he may return. I'll see you this evening.'

By that Saturday evening she had opened the door and stepped out into the snicket. She showed Peter the result of her work.

'Now we need not be quite so circumspect in visiting you,' he said with a broad smile. 'You really are a remarkable young queen.'

Lucy gave him a little curtsy. She looked quizzically at Peter. She knew that if she had been Elspeth she would have given him a lovely kiss on his open honest face, but she just could not. She contented herself with a smile.

The Sunday and Monday passed quite quickly as Lucy became more and more involved in her writing. There was still no report of the Earl of Bardsey's return, but preparations for the coronation were proceeding.

On the Tuesday Peter arrived with news.

'My father has learnt that there is an English ship in the roads. It will dock with this evening's tide. It will need to discharge its cargo and load a fresh one so it should sail the day after tomorrow. If we leave here at four on that morning you can be aboard and on the high seas by six. If you are dressed as a friar it will not arouse suspicion. They are often out and about early. Then within a couple of days you will be safe at King Henry's court in England.'

That day Lucy finished her treatise and took a fresh sheet of paper and wrote:

Declaration.

The rules by which a nation should be governed.

She summarised all her thoughts onto the one side and read it through and sat back with a sense of satisfaction. So that was how a nation should be ruled.

But of course it was not going to happen.

She must face the truth. No doubt there would be some muted opposition to the prince as king, but he would have all the power and authority of the throne. Suppose she got to England. Was there any chance King Henry, with all his other domestic problems, would help her regain her throne? Her existence in England might embarrass the prince after he had announced her death, but it was unlikely to lead to a revolt.

And suppose it did. Did she want a civil war with the deaths of hundreds, perhaps thousands, of the very people she wanted to serve? The general populace would decide they must just accept things as they were. They would live in fear. They would turn a blind eye to his arbitrary justice and his harsh rule. In time Ferdinand's ambitions would be fulfilled when Lady Barbara succeeded. They would have won. And all she would have was a small pile of paper.

She looked at her documents and, for the first time since the time of her father's death, she began to sob.

It was with a heavy heart she climbed into the manger, but she could not sleep. In two days she would probably be safely away. Then what? A useless life at the court of a King with a reputation for ruthlessness little different from Prince Rupert's lay ahead of her. She would have failed her father, her people and her own ideals.

Chapter 34

'LET THE BOAT SAIL'

On the Wednesday morning Peter arrived by way of the snicket accompanied by Henry Martley.

'We met in the square.' Peter explained.

'My father and the earl have not yet returned. My mother is beginning to worry some calamity has befallen them,' Henry said.

Lucy decided not to relay her fears. It would serve no purpose.

'Peter tells me he has some amazing news for you. He felt I too should hear it.'

'Lucy,' said Peter breathlessly, 'what I have to tell you is almost unbelievable. Last night Brother Simon was strong enough to go to Mass at St. Stephano's. When the time came, he went up to take the host and, of course, he knelt at the altar rail. The archbishop came to him and bent to give him the bread. Brother Simon looked up and saw the great pectoral cross of the archbishop swing into his line of sight. Suddenly his memory of the dreadful afternoon of your father's death cleared. He remembered the moment that he was struck down by the knight with a crest of yellow plumes. That man had swinging from his neck a great gold medallion. The medallion of a Black Dog, the prince's emblem.'

'But,' said Henry, 'that means it must have been Ferdinand. He wore that medallion at all times. Is that possible? Is that really possible Peter? Can you remember the details of those terrible minutes that led up to your finding the king?'

Peter said slowly, 'Well, I rode to get the wine Brother Simon requested. On the way I passed the prince. He was alone, I remember thinking that was a bit odd. Usually he would have his squire with him. It took me ages to find the steward and when I returned with him, the prince was mounted but had hardly budged. But now he had Ferdinand and Montelucca with him. I remember thinking Ferdinand must have captured the count. Another thing, I don't think Montelucca had his helmet on. No. I'm sure he didn't.'

'Well, in that case how did you know it was Montelucca?' Henry interrupted.

'I don't know how. I just knew it was him.' Peter frowned as he tried to think back. 'The strange thing is I was absolutely sure.' He paused again. 'I remember. His helmet with his yellow feathers was there. But he was not wearing it. Ferdinand was holding it. Yes, that's how I knew it was Montelucca.'

'Go on. What happened next?' Henry pressed.

'Then, when we reached the clearing, there was this soldier who saw the killing. He was positive the killer was wearing Montelucca's helmet. And as he was dying, the poor King said the same. So everyone believed it was him. Until Brother Simon told me what happened, I still assumed it was Montelucca. Now that I think about it, I can see it did not have to be him. It just never crossed my mind that the king was murdered. We were in the middle of a battle. If someone is killed, you take it for granted it's by the enemy.'

He paused then added, 'Anyway, why would Montelucca do it? He had no loyalty to either side. Doubtless, once he knew of Voravia's victory, he would be planning to offer his services back to King Charles. But he would not have been shy of lending his helmet to Ferdinand for a price. That man would do anything for money.'

'My father was killed by Ferdinand! No, it's impossible. Even he would not be such a traitor!'

'Yes, I'm sure he was. It explains everything. How could Montelucca do it? He had neither motive nor much opportunity. I've been a naïve fool not to reason out the truth.'

'Ferdinand certainly struck the blow but I am sure the prince was behind it. He planned the murder of his own brother,' Henry said. He paused for a moment then added. 'And, of course, Montelucca had to be silenced. He knew Ferdinand had borrowed the helmet. We can be sure that, having got in so deep, they won't hesitate to kill again and again.'

'I'm sure that's true.' Peter was still shaking his head at the logic of what had happened.

'You know,' said Henry thoughtfully, 'I think Ferdinand had crossed that dreadful threshold earlier. I doubt I was the only one troubled by the cause of Montague's death. But, with a battle imminent, no one wanted to spend time investigating the matter. Brother Simon said he carried a bruise to his head. I think Ferdinand knocked him out then hanged him.'

'Oh no! His decent act on my behalf led to his death.' Peter sat down heavily on Lucy's stool. 'Poor, poor Richard. If he hadn't had the courage to tell the truth of what happened at the bridge he'd be alive today and I'd be but a foot soldier.'

'That may be true. And if you had been, you would never have been able to tell my father of your idea to cover the brook. Doubtless Sloronia would have triumphed and probably the pair of us, together with thousands more, would have died in a battle we were destined to lose,' Henry pointed out. 'You could say our nation was saved by Montague's honesty. That's not a bad memorial.'

There was a silence as the enormity of all the crimes sank in. Then Lucy turned to face the others.

'I am not going to England. Let the boat sail. It goes without me. I shall fight my father's and the duke's murderers. If I lose and perish I will, at least, have done my best. I owe it to my dear papa.'

As she said these words she felt an enormous sense of relief. The horrible feeling of helplessness that had borne down on her for the last twenty-four hours lifted. She looked at her friends and thought that she would not have changed them for a thousand men-at-arms.

'But what have we got to fight with? We are just the three of us against the full might of the state?'

Lucy guessed that Peter was probably thinking that, when it came to actually fighting, there was really only he alone.

'Well to start with, can't Brother Simon go and

tell the archbishop?' Lucy asked.

'Yes, he could and perhaps he should. But do you think the archbishop will believe him? Why didn't he come forward earlier? It'll be the word of a humble friar against the man who will be King in two days' time. Furthermore, if he is not believed it will go very badly for him,' Henry Martley said thoughtfully.

'I agree with you, Henry. Anyway Brother Simon would be terrified of addressing a man like Archbishop Godwin in person. We would have to get him to write down his accusation and give it to the archbishop.' Peter said.

'And would he read it do you think? I mean any troublemaker could write out something similar. We need to convince him it is genuine, really genuine. Really what it needs, is for it to be sealed.' Henry said.

'How strange,' murmured Lucy, 'the discovery of the Great Seal has become as important to us as to the prince.'

'I doubt it will trouble him for long, once he is crowned.' said Henry. 'He'll be able to declare King Charles' seal lost in battle and have a new one minted in his name. But if we had it, it would certainly give us a huge advantage for a few days. Peter, when exactly was the last time you saw it?'

'It was towards the end of the battle. When it was obvious the victory was won. King Charles called our men off to prevent any more slaughter. He wrote a note to the Sloronians and sealed it. I saw him do that.'

'So he saw hardly anyone after that?'

'No. I suppose it could have fallen on the battlefield, but I doubt it. For one thing King Charles always wore it round his neck and for another the scavengers would have found it.'

'That's true and if one of them did they would have claimed Tuscade's reward.' Lucy remembered the prince's outburst all those weeks ago.

'So someone still has it,' said Henry.

'Well, we know he did not give it to the prince, or to the duke - he would surely have used it against the prince. He did not give it to my father or to the Earl of Bardsey.'

'He couldn't have done so. He saw none of them until he was dying. Yet he said, most clearly, that it was with his most trusted friend.' Peter frowned in concentration.

The three of them stood in thought.

There was a stillness in the tack room, broken only by the occasional movement of the great warhorse in his stable.

Suddenly Henry and Peter said as one. 'Of course, it's Stang!'

'Stang! Yes, it's obvious. Who did my dear father trust more than his old companion?' Lucy was bright-eyed with excitement.

'Peter, can you remember which armour, which harness Stang had on that day?' Henry asked excitedly.

'Of course.' Peter was already over by the racks.

'This is it.' He heaved a huge saddle down onto

the floor and turned it over, he ran his hand beneath the leather flaps and gave a cry of triumph.

Peter pulled out a gold chain. Attached to the end was a heavy ring and, set into the face of the ring, a ruby with the intaglio royal seal of Voravia.

Lucy felt a rush of exhilaration. Now they had a weapon to fight with. She needed a breath of fresh air. She lifted the latch to the door and stepped outside into the snicket. Peter and Henry found her leaning against the wall, looking up at the azure sky, a small smile hovering about her lips.

'The coronation takes place on Saturday, you say? That's in two days' time.'

Peter nodded.

'Once the archbishop learns the truth, he will have to call off the ceremony. He was against the prince becoming protector. I learnt that from Flanders. So he will not take much persuading. The prince doesn't hold quite all the power in Voravia. If the Church does not accept him, we have a powerful ally. Return here this evening with Brother Simon's deposition, I'll sign and seal it. Then be here with Elspeth early tomorrow. Tell her to bring her needle and Brother Simon's robe. We can fashion something out of it. I need to show myself to the archbishop once he has seen the deposition. When I do that, I want to look a bit more, well, more regal.'

Chapter 35

BLOOD IN THE WAX

From very early the following morning Lucy could hear great activity in the stable yard, as preparations for the morrow's coronation of King Rupert got under way. Horses would have to be groomed and harness polished. Caparisons would be brought out from the castle in readiness for the procession.

Peter brought Elspeth and Abigail to the snicket door and Lucy let the women in. He returned so as to make his regular entrance through the main gate.

'I explained to my father you were determined to stay and fight the prince. He did start to object and say you were too young and that you should flee to England but then he changed his mind and told me that I could have no better use for my Toledo blade than to use it in your cause. I think he was being rather romantic. I explained that it was the archbishop who is more likely to save us, not my steel.'

'And I wanted to help,' said Abigail. 'I bought some lace and also a pair of shoes in the market from a trader from England. We can add the lace to the dress. Also here are some gloves of mine. They are not of the highest fashion but I think they will be better than none.'

Abigail and Elspeth set to work to turn the black and white friar's garb into a simple but elegant dress. They added the lace and by midday Lucy had tried it on for size. With the lace cuffs and collar and the crimson shoes she looked very much the princess.

'Let's now wash you tresses and in the morning Elspeth can brush them until they shine.' Lucy could see that Abigail was enjoying the challenge of making her look as regal as possible given their restricted means.

'I expect you like having Elspeth with you, Abigail.' Lucy asked.

'Why, of course, but can you believe it, all she wants to do is to learn from my William? Proper little scholar she has become. If all the girls in Voravia take after you and her what will become of us? Who will do the cooking, who will mend the clothes, who will clean the house and who will nurse the babies? It isn't natural for women to become educated. Oh it's different for you, my lady, you're a princess and, I hopes, soon a queen.'

Lucy laughed, 'Oh Abigail, when I am queen, things will be rather different. I have been spending my time deciding on how I want Voravia to change. Everyone, peasant, farmer, trader, noble and, yes, royalty will be equal before the law. Women shall have the same rights as men. The whole world is changing, as your good William taught me, and it must change for the poor and the weak as much as for the rich and the powerful. See, I have written it all down here in the declaration I shall make as soon as I am queen.'

Lucy showed Abigail the sheaf of papers she had prepared.

'You wrote all that, it's amazing, Lucy, I mean Queen Lucia. Of course I long for you to bring these dreadful times to an end but I do worry a bit about how people like me will manage in the new world you will have us live in. Elspeth will be fine. She's quite a convert to the new learning. It's amazing, a simple farmer's lass!'

The women left at midday and Lucy changed from her fine dress into her plain shift. She read through her declaration and made a few small changes.

In the late afternoon Peter and Henry arrived, accompanied by Brother Simon who was very nervous. Since Lucy had taken his friar's habit, he had made a replacement from some cloth Abigail had bought.

'Now, Brother Simon, let me read what you have written. Then I shall address it to the archbishop, add my signature and affix the Great Seal of Voravia. When the archbishop sees that he will be sure to read it.'

The friar took from his tunic a sheet of parchment and passed it to Lucy.

She read: '*I Brother Simon of the Dominican Order do hereby make this deposition that I solemnly declare to be the entire truth. I was present at the battle in the snow on the feast of St. Agatha in the year of Our Lord 1535. I was in attendance on the army of King Charles IV of Voravia...'* She read on. Even though Peter had told her of Brother Simon's revelation, she still found it almost impossible to believe that her half-uncle had arranged the killing of her father.

'It is well written, as I would expect from so good

a scholar as you, Brother. Now let us fold it and seal it. Peter, please light the candle and we will allow it to drip here, I think the document will look most authentic if it is sealed in wax.' Lucy indicated the place.

The candle was lit and Peter held it over the parchment. When the first pool of hot wax fell, Henry leant forward, drew the sharp point of the chisel across the ball of his thumb and squeezed some drops of blood into the wax. Lucy carefully pressed the seal down and withdrew it. The familiar crest with its swans and King Charles' initials almost glowed back from the scarlet wax.

Then she wrote: *To the Cardinal Archbishop Godwin.*

I, Lucia, as yet uncrowned Queen of Voravia, request that you immediately read this deposition, written by Brother Simon, my tutor. Signed and sealed this twenty-first day of March 1535. I shall present myself to you presently.

She signed her name and wrote beneath it *Lucia Regina.*

'Brother Simon take this to the Cathedral at the first opportunity, but on no account excite the suspicion of the soldiers. Good luck.'

Brother Simon slipped out of the door and into the snicket.

Lucy went over to her desk.

'Now, gentlemen, I should be pleased if you would witness my signature to my document. This shall be my rule. It will be read in all the churches once I am queen so that every citizen will know his rights and duties, and I will know mine.'

Once more the Great Seal was affixed and Lucy signed the declaration and Peter and Henry added their names as witnesses.

She placed the papers in a small pile on the bench.

As evening drew on, Peter went to groom Belle. Henry took a single sheet of folded paper from his doublet and handed it to Lucy with a small smile. She opened it. It was a sonnet entitled '*A war betwixt the heart and the head.*'

'I wrote it on the eve of the great battle,' he explained bashfully.

Lucy read the lines, it was a love poem and as she read she began to chew her lip. Henry seemed to have poured his soul into the lines. She read them through a second time. It was a complicated poem. A casual reader would enjoy the clever use of words and images, but to Lucy there was another way of reading the sentiments, they spoke of passion and longing. The final couplet read;

The victory's won. The victor counts his cost;

For though the heart did triumph yet to thee 'tis lost.

'Thank you, Henry, it's lovely. It shall live close to my heart.'

She refolded the paper and tucked it into her bodice. This was by no means the first such sonnet Henry had written for her. She suspected the poet sometimes wrote as much to demonstrate his talent as to pledge his faithfulness. On at least two occasions there had been a hidden message contained in the first letter of each line. In the first one of these acrostics, the letters spelt *my heart is thine,* a rather banal sentiment, Lucy thought. The second had been much more intimate, if Lucy correctly understood Henry's reference. She had secreted that poem away, fearful that it might be found and read. These acrostic poems had been something of a rage at King Charles' court.

As darkness drew on the three of them settled down for the night. Lucy lay in the manger smiling at the contrast between her two swains; one who would win her with his sword and his body, the other with his pen and his mind. The rivals and friends lay side by side in the straw. Stang stood there quietly, watching over them.

Chapter 36

OUR ONLY CHANCE

On the morning of the coronation of King Rupert, the three sleepers in the stable woke as the sun rose and waited impatiently for Brother Simon. He arrived with Elspeth, her curls now restored to their former dazzling copper, shortly after six.

'Oh Elspeth, you look gorgeous, but wasn't that a terrible risk? You might easily have been recognized.' Peter asked.

'No, the streets are full of people. I was lost in the crowd. The prince has ordered everyone to line the route from the castle to the main square. There'll be trouble for anyone staying at home.'

Brother Simon was in a terrible state of worry.

'Princess, I have failed you. How can I possibly say how sorry I am?' The man was close to tears.

'Now, sit down, and tell us what happened. Do they know where I am hid?' Lucy tried to remain calm as she showed Simon the makeshift chair.

Brother Simon took a deep breath and then said, 'No, there I did not fail you. But in everything else, I did. I went to the archbishop's palace and had a great deal of difficulty in persuading the doorkeeper to let me in. I was shown to a waiting room and had to wait for hours. I can't think why as there was only a mother superior and a novitiate in front of me. Eventually I was shown through, but not to see the archbishop, to see his secretary.' Brother Simon paused and looked beseechingly at the three young faces in front of him. 'He was a dreadful man. No credit to our Church. Probably a rich man's son who lives well on the tithes of the poor. I began to explain that I had a deposition that would make the coronation unlawful and that it was sealed by Queen Lucia. He interrupted me to say that the queen was dead. He didn't believe me. Anyway, he said, the archbishop was far too busy with the preparations for the coronation. I asked if he would give my document to the archbishop and he said he might, but not until after the ceremony.'

'Did you hand it to him?' Henry asked.

'No, what would be the point? Then I asked him, and I was desperate, what could I do? He said in a sarcastic sort of way I could raise an objection at the time of the coronation. But he said I would probably be arrested as a madman and it would bring disgrace on my order. With that he dismissed me. Oh princess, I have been as feeble as ever.'

'Rubbish, you were brave to even try, and you have learned something of value. Let me think.' Lucy knitted her brows. She must think. In a matter of hours Prince Rupert would be King. He would take his time in hunting them down, but time was one thing he would not be short of. The story of the burning of Joan of Arc had always seemed so terrible. Now, as a witch, she too would die in the same ghastly way. She felt her brain assailed by all sorts of ideas and snatched recollections. For a second or two she wondered whether there was a chance the boat for England would still be in the harbour. But, of course, it would have left on the tide. Oh why hadn't she followed William's advice? Why, why? She fought back her panic. She was shivering.

What was it Peter had said? William was being romantic. But so had Flanders been, and Peter and even poor Vladimar. And so had so many when she had walked behind her father's coffin. That day the streets were full, as they would be today. She took a deep breath. An idea began to form in her mind.

'I think we have but one chance,' she began. Initially she was quite hesitant but as she progressed she became more confident. Her panic was gone. She finished by saying that everything would depend on their getting their timing absolutely right.

When she had finished there was a long silence. Then Peter nodded and said, 'I agree, it's our only hope.'

'I think you should accompany Brother Simon. If there is any fighting to be done, it will be in the Nieu Square. I can't imagine anyone will be able to stand a chance against you.' She gave Peter a radiant smile. It was the sort any soldier would carry joyfully into battle. 'But first I would like you and Henry to prepare the horses.'

Chapter 37

A CAUSE

Peter and Henry busied themselves for the next hour with grooming and saddling-up Stang, Belle and Tench. Then Peter strapped on his fine sword and he and Brother Simon made their way out of the snicket. He tried to convey to the friar, who was palpably terrified, a sense of confidence. It was only an act. He was almost as nervous himself.

The streets were thronged with citizens. There were soldiers under the command of sergeants trying to shepherd the populace into place. Some were being organized to line the street; others were being herded down to the Nieu Square to witness the crowning of the new king. Peter arrived at his parents' house. William and Abigail were standing outside. He pulled them to one side, away from the soldiers, and spoke quietly and urgently to them.

'You must help us. It's our only chance.'

First he explained the role his father should play. William agreed enthusiastically.

Then he turned to his mother. 'Mother, come with me. Everything's going to depend on you. Lucy says she knows we can rely on you.'

Abigail did not appear to notice that her son did not seem quite to share Lucy's confidence. She followed Peter and Brother Simon through the crowds to the end of the street where it emptied into the main square. This was to be Abigail's post.

'As soon as the last of the prince's retinue passes - but not before - you must hurry back to the stable yard. Henry will be waiting for you. Tell him he may leave. You can do that?'

'Yes, if I have to fight my way there, I'll do it.' There was a determination in Abigail's tone that Peter had forgotten. Lucy had been right. They could depend on her.

Peter and Brother Simon pushed their way through the swelling crowds and into the square.

In front of the great cathedral's west end, with its three-hundred-year-old carvings, a dais had been set up. On it were two altars. Resting on the one to the left were the state crown and the sceptre. As Peter watched, three workmen staggered out of a side door with a heavy oriental carpet that they unrolled before the altars. Above the dais was a canopy that bucked and rattled in the stiff breeze. The pale blue and white pennants at its four corners streamed out, cracking in the wind.

Peter looked out and down to the estuary towards the narrows across which, in times of danger, the great chains would be drawn. The fresh breeze had whipped the sea into waves, their tops blown off in white horses. He could see three merchantmen lying at anchor in the Roads. They were waiting for the tide to turn and sweep them into the harbour on the rising water.

The great bell of St. Stephano's began to peal.

Peter's chest was constricting with worry. He was not too concerned about the part he had to play. If the worst came to the worst, he would fight. It was the enormous risk Lucy was to take. She had to time her move precisely. If she came too soon, the soldiers would be able to seize her. If she left it too late, the prince would have all the power of a crowned monarch. Brother Simon must delay matters long enough for the retinue to have cleared the streets and be in the square. So much depended upon Abigail. Would she panic and not carry out her part? Would the crowds be too dense for her to get to Henry in time?

His father would start the shouts of 'Queen Lucia' loudly enough, he felt sure, but would the crowd join in? Lucy had only two weapons. One was Henry's sword. Peter had enormous respect and affection for his friend and rival in love but, he had to admit, he was not much of a fighter. The other was Lucy's personality. Was her confidence in the crowd's reaction justified? In the end everything would depend on the force of a fifteen-year-old girl's leadership qualities and the display of her courage.

If they failed they could expect no mercy from the prince or Ferdinand. There would be no trials. They would burn Lucy as a witch. He and Henry would hang. Would he have to support and comfort Henry as they faced their terrible ordeal? What Tuscade and Ferdinand would do to Elspeth was probably beyond imagining.

The centre door to the cathedral was flung open and Archbishop Godwin stepped through, accompanied by two bishops and three or four attendant chaplains. He wore an alb of the finest linen, secured at the waist by a cincture. Over this was a chasuble, then a magnificent cope of purple and aquamarine embroidered with gold thread. On his head, and in some danger of being snatched away by the breeze, he wore a mitre and in his hand he carried his crosier. He went to the right-hand altar and laid on it a heavy tome. Peter assumed this bore the words of the coronation ceremony.

A ragged cheer began to flow down the street from the castle. It was hardly enthusiastic, thought Peter, more one of duty. The prince's party must be on its way.

Peter edged his way to the front of the crowd, pulling the friar with him. A line of pikemen stood to hold the crowd back. He clutched the deposition firmly in his right hand as his heart pounded. His mouth was dry.

A fanfare of trumpets announced the arrival in the square of Sir Ferdinand le Gray followed by Prince Rupert on a superbly caparisoned warhorse led by the Earl of Flytte. Behind him rode a hugely fat young man, who Peter took to be the Earl of Tuscade and a woman, presumably the prince's daughter, Lady Barbara, of whom Elspeth had frequently spoken. All were dressed in their finest court clothes. Finally came a contingent of about fifty foot soldiers wearing chain mail and polished steel breastplates, under the command of the High Constable, Sir Hugh Montague.

The party approached the dais and Prince Rupert dismounted. He stepped forward and bowed to the archbishop.

Archbishop Godwin came to the front and rapped his crosier three times to command silence. 'Nobles and citizens of Voravia,' he began, 'we are gathered here to witness the coronation of the high and mighty Prince Rupert as sovereign of Voravia and its supplicant principalities and dukedoms. The sacrament of coronation is a solemn contract between ruler and ruled. It acknowledges the power and responsibilities of the one and the entitlements and obligations of the other.'

'Before I proceed to the crowning of the new monarch I am required to ask if anyone present knows of any just cause or impediment as to why this said prince may not be crowned King of Voravia he do now present it, or forever keep his silence. For know you well that, once crowned, such objection shall be treated as high treason.'

There was a pause.

The archbishop was about to begin when Peter gave Brother Simon a dig in the ribs.

'I have a just cause,' the friar said, not very loudly.

Peter pushed through the startled pikemen in front of him pulling Brother Simon after him. They advanced towards the party before the archbishop.

'We have a cause. We have a just cause.' Peter shouted and turned to see three soldiers begin to advance towards him.

Chapter 38

THE SCAR

He recognised Sergeant Watts.

'Sergeant, please help me. The queen is still alive.'

'Wait, lads,' Ben Watts barked. ''Tis Squire Peter. He be a fine soldier.'

Peter seized his chance. Dragging the nervous friar by the hand, he reached the dais.

There was a hubbub in the square; people were shouting.

'Tell the archbishop, Brother, tell him,' Peter shouted.

'I accuse Sir Ferdinand le Gray of the murder of King Charles IV and Prince Rupert of being complicit in that crime,' Brother Simon managed to gasp out.

'Ridiculous, he's a madman, take him away!' Prince Rupert said in a quiet hard voice.

'This is Brother Simon's testament. It is witnessed by the lawful heir to King Charles - his daughter Princess Lucia - and sealed by her with the Great Seal of Voravia. It is addressed to you, my Lord, and signed in her own hand.' Peter offered the parchment to the astonished archbishop.

Peter could see the archbishop struggling with his dilemma. Would he read the document or ignore it and proceed with the ceremony?

Sir Ferdinand stepped forward and made to seize it. 'You, Peter Salt, I should have had you disposed of months ago.'

Suddenly Brother Simon ripped open his habit. 'Your grace, here is the wound that man inflicted on me.'

The sight of the dreadful scar settled the matter.

'Allow me to see the testament. Pass it to me.'

The archbishop took the document.

'Pray, Prince Rupert, do you recognise this seal?'

'It's a counterfeit. Anyone could make that.'

'I think not or you would have done so. As I understand it your rule has been plagued by your inability to seal orders in council,' the archbishop said, almost as an aside.

He broke the seal and read. Peter could see him mouth the words of the accusation. Then he turned and pointed at Sir Ferdinand.

'And that is the medallion you saw, Brother?'

'Yes, your grace.'

'This accusation is so serious, Brother, I must demand of you that you swear by Almighty God that it is the complete truth.'

'I swear,' Brother Simon replied.

'Of course it's a complete sham! Everyone knows Princess Lucia is dead. A very sad event, but, regrettably, true. Her body lies in the royal vault at Voravine. Now let us proceed.'

Prince Rupert tossed the testament to the carpet but, even as he did so, a shout came from the end of the street towards the castle. Further shouts and cheers followed. The party at the dais turned and watched as a growing tumult of sound began to roll down towards them. The noise grew louder and now they could pick out individual words, 'Long Live Queen Lucia!' 'God save Princess Lucy!' 'Down with the prince!'

The crowd in the square started to surge towards the spot where the mob was thronging. There were laughs and taunts thrown at the prince where he stood transfixed.

Peter stepped up onto the dais. From this vantage point he looked back towards the action. He could see up the street that led from the palace.

Henry Martley, dressed in his squire's attire and riding Belle, pushed forward between the excited crowds. He was shouting, 'Make way for Queen Lucia, rightful Queen of Voravia! Make way!'

He was followed by Lucy sitting high on Stang's huge back. She was wearing the plain black and white dress that Abigail and Elspeth had fashioned from the Dominican friar's robe. Around her neck hung the Great Seal of Voravia. Her back was as straight as a lance, her shining golden tresses held in place by a white silk band round her brow but fluttering around her shoulders in the breeze, her head and gaze high, her solemn oval face was that of one determined to rule. She looked as light as a bird. It seemed impossible that one so slight could challenge the power of the prince. Yet she had about her an aura of steel, that mysterious strength that is the talisman of leadership. Some women had run into their homes and were throwing flowers from the upper windows. Men, doubtless recalling their own daughters and, as Lucy had calculated, overcome by the romance of the beautiful young queen, were choking back their tears. Everywhere there was an outpouring of affection and hope.

'It may be difficult to prove the veracity of the friar's testament but it should not be too difficult to recognise the royal princess,' said the archbishop as Henry and Belle forced their way into the square.

They had no retinue, just the queen's sole lady-in-waiting, Elspeth, mounted on Tench and beaming and waving to the crowd, her mass of curls bouncing around her jolly face.

Henry rode slowly towards the soldiers formed up between them and the prince. Behind him the crowds surged around Stang, shouting, cheering and laughing.

The archbishop turned a furious face to the prince. 'Prince Rupert, it has been alleged that the death of King Charles was caused by your squire. Until I am sure that this allegation is false I shall not proceed. Furthermore, it would seem that I was scandalously misled as to the death of the Princess Lucia. Pending my consideration of the friar's allegations I require the pair of you to surrender yourselves to justice.'

'This is outrageous!' shouted Prince Rupert, but he knew he was beaten.

Peter saw him look for a second at the crown. That badge of majesty, for which he had longed and schemed and killed. He would never be closer to it than now. He had been beaten by a mere wisp of a girl. A girl who had no army and no weapons of war. Just her courage and the love of the people. Peter could barely believe that she had done it.

'Let's get out of here!'

Ferdinand turned his horse. It collided with that of his fiancée, Lady Barbara, who put out a restraining hand, and shouted:

'It's not true. Say it's not true.'

'Get out of the way, you stupid bitch.'

Ferdinand kicked his horse into a canter. It slithered and skittered across the cobbles towards the road that led out of the square and down towards the port. The prince, realizing that the game was lost, mounted his horse and he and Tuscade fled after Ferdinand.

Sir Hugh Montague stood flabbergasted at the turn of events. He could have heard but little of the archbishop's words with the prince and, probably still feeling obliged to defend the existing order, began to move towards Peter.

Peter spun round and shouted, 'Sir Hugh, Ferdinand le Gray killed not only King Charles but also murdered your son Richard. We must avenge both those deaths.'

'I'll catch them,' yelled Henry.

He dug in his heels and sent Belle after the fleeing killers. Sir Hugh, now realising that Ferdinand's flight was explained by his guilt, began to organise a pursuit. Peter could see that his men, encumbered by their armour and without horses, would be of little immediate help. For a second he thought of lifting Lucy down from Stang and taking her place. But he had never ridden side-saddle and now was no time to try to learn.

'We must help Henry,' Lucy shouted and she and

Elspeth turned their mounts and set off after Henry.

Peter sprang after the horses. They were heading for the harbour. They would have to take the main road that swung round in a loop to avoid the cliff that lay between the city and the port. He would use one of the steep paths that led straight down.

Running, often jumping, down the steps, his sword slapping his leg, he raced down, passing the little terraced vegetable plots that clung to the hillside.

He rounded a corner and the harbour came into view. He could see Ferdinand, already dismounted and running along the quayside. Prince Rupert and Tuscade came into view and close behind them Henry Martley, riding Belle as if in a horserace.

'Just delay them, Henry,' Peter said to himself, 'just a few minutes.'

The lane twisted left and Peter lost sight of the quay for a few moments. When he next saw it, he beheld a scene of chaos. The prince and Tuscade were off their mounts with their weapons drawn, as was Henry who was bravely parrying each thrust. Le Gray had found a small fishing vessel, straining at its mooring ropes as the ebbing tide sucked the water from the harbour. He was starting to cast off the stern warp.

Peter saw Elspeth appear on Tench. She was riding the pony at full gallop. She must have overtaken the more cumbersome Stang on the descent. A moment later Lucy, on Stang, followed.

Then he saw Henry take a savage blow to the thigh and fall. His sword clattered to the ground. The prince stepped forward to kill him.

Chapter 39

EBB TIDE

'No, no,' shouted Lucy.

For a second the prince paused. Elspeth hurled herself from Tench and crashed into the prince. The shock knocked him back. Lucy dismounted and bent over the writhing Henry. His hose was already crimson with blood.

Peter reached a low wall. He sprang up on to it. There was a twenty-foot drop below him to a small seaweed-strewn beach. He turned to his left, in the direction of the quay, and raced along, his fear of heights forgotten. A few more seconds and he would be able to jump down to the flat land beside the harbour. He saw Ferdinand had stopped and was re-mooring the vessel.

'Bring her here,' Ferdinand shouted. 'Get her on the boat.'

If they could capture the princess, they would have a priceless hostage to bargain with. He saw Ferdinand begin to race back towards the struggle, evidently unaware of Peter's imminent arrival.

Lucy was fighting. The prince and Tuscade started half carrying, half dragging her along the quay. For a moment she managed to grab a bollard, but they wrenched her free. Then he saw Elspeth once more spring into the fight. She grabbed the prince by the arm and Peter saw her sink her teeth into his wrist.

'Bitch, you little bitch,' he yelled and, releasing

his grip on Lucy, hurled Elspeth to the ground. She fell on her face at the feet of Tuscade. Peter saw the earl bend over the sprawling Elspeth, take her by the collar of her bodice and pull her head back up close to his. He drew his dagger.

He's going to slit her throat, Peter thought.

'I'll cut you to shreds, you trash. When I've finished with you, you'll weep whenever you see your mutilated face in a glass. No man will look at you without loathing. You'll wish I'd finished you off!' Tuscade shouted, his face contorted with malice.

Only yards away from the drop to the quay, Peter saw Tuscade raise his blade to slash at Elspeth's face. He did it quite slowly as he savoured the moment. Then suddenly he let out a howl of pain, dropped his knife and clutched his leg as Elspeth rolled clear.

'My leg, my ulcer, oh my God!' Tuscade cried.

Peter saw Elspeth, still on her knees, had a short length of mooring rope in her hands. She must have managed to swing it into Tuscade's calf. Now she hit him again with all her might on the same spot. In agony he staggered into Stang's rump. The great warhorse gave a startled neigh, shied and lashed out with his hind leg. The huge iron-shod hoof caught Tuscade on the temple. He was dead before his swollen body hit the ground.

'Come on. Help me with the girl!' le Gray shouted.

Peter leapt down. He was on the quay, his sword in his hand.

Le Gray made a last effort to carry Lucy, then

turned and fled. For a few moments the prince stood, transfixed by the fearful sight of his son's shattered skull, then turned to follow le Gray.

Peter looked ahead. Le Gray had freed one of the warps. The fishing boat's stern swung out on the current. The bow mooring pulled tight as a bowstring.

The prince raced along the quay as le Gray began to hack at the bow painter with his sword.

Peter saw Prince Rupert arrive at the mooring as the painter gave. He made a despairing leap for the boat. His hands grabbed the gunwale and his feet splashed into the water. He hung there trying to pull himself aboard.

Peter re-sheathed his sword and stooped down to see if Lucy or Elspeth were injured. They were on their knees, panting from their exertions. He moved towards Henry, horrified by the blood.

'We are not in the least damaged. We'll see to Henry. Don't let them escape, the murderers,' Lucy gasped.

'They won't,' Peter shouted over his shoulder as he sprang onto Belle and sent her down the quay.

The boat, adrift but with no steerage, was being swept towards the narrow entrance to the harbour as Peter drew alongside. It crashed into the stonework of the jetty, crushing Prince Rupert of Heinz-Coburg as if he were made of straw. He fell, limp as a doll, into the ebbing water. Within seconds the boat would be clear.

'Come on Belle, come on my brave friend,' Peter

whispered in his mare's ear and, as if clearing the tree trunk on the foreshore, she jumped across the widening gap into the fast-moving vessel and onto the sails bundled in the hold amidships. Her momentum brought her to her knees and Peter was off and advancing towards the astonished le Gray.

Le Gray realizing that his efforts with the tiller were useless, the boat was at the mercy of the tide, picked up his sword for a final fight.

The vessel was now clear of the harbour and, caught in the fast ebb tide, was swept into the first of the moored merchantmen and then on towards the breakers on the bar to the estuary. Belle, back on her feet, her eyes wide in fear of the water, was motionless in the hold.

'You, Salt, you jumped-up tradesman's son, you've ruined my life, now I'm going to kill you,' le Gray engaged Peter's sword and tried to twist it aside.

The blades slithered across each other. Peter once again felt the red mist of combat haze his vision. This time he would kill le Gray. He parried le Gray's thrust with ease and lunged. His lovely Toledo steel sliced through le Gray's doublet and into his right arm. Le Gray rocked back. His heel caught in a loose rope. He tripped sideways, lost his balance and fell to his knees, his sword hand on the deck. Peter stepped forward and brought his foot down hard on le Gray's wrist. The sword clattered free. With one kick Peter sent it overboard. Le Gray looked up. His eyes no longer cold with arrogance but glazed with the knowledge he was going to die. Peter paused. Then he heard Belle, terrified of the water, neigh with fear. He could not; he must not kill in cold blood.

He turned, jumped down into the well, ran past Belle and up the steps to the foredeck. He dropped his sword to the deck.

'Quick come and help me with the anchor or we'll all be drowned,' Peter shouted as he fought to free the anchor from the foresail that lay across it. He dragged the sail aside as the ship struck the last of the moored vessels and headed towards the crashing waves, the roar of the water now thundering in his ears.

He had begun to free the anchor chain from its cleat when something caused him to look round. He saw le Gray as the razor-sharp gutting knife began its upwards thrust at his belly. As Peter hurled himself sideways the ship struck. There was a shuddering jar. Le Gray had to grab the gunwale. The boat was lifted by a huge breaker and dropped with a shattering crash on the bar. It heeled over and the next wave pounded over the side and into the well. He heard the ballast shift as the following wave crashed onboard. There was a momentary lull. Peter, on his hands and knees looked up. Le Gray, drenched and staring death by drowning, crawled towards him, the knife still clutched in his hand. Then, with a terrible crash, a huge wave slammed into and over the stricken vessel. Peter saw le Gray picked up by a wall of water and swept overboard. The next wave broke the vessel's back. The mast hung for a split second over him then collapsed in a tangle of halyards and shrouds over the side. The boat was on her beam-ends, her timbers disintegrating. Peter struggled to his feet. He was standing on the taffrail, the deck reared vertically above him. No one, save a few fishermen, knew how to swim. He was going to drown.

Another torrent of breaking surf lifted him clear and flung him into the cauldron of water. He lashed out frantically. The next moment he received a terrific blow to the head from a loose spar. He went down, the water closed over his head. He gasped and his lungs filled with water. He flailed out and his right hand hit a loose thong of leather, instinctively he grabbed it and pulled with all his strength. Another wave slammed into him and almost broke his grasp. He hung on and, in the gap before the next wave, managed to engage his left hand. He rode out the following deluge and opening his eyes saw Belle's head close to his. He had hold of her loose reins.

Peter pulled himself close to the horse until he could grip her mane; she was swimming steadily for the beach. Three minutes later her feet had hit the sand and she dragged the exhausted Peter out of the raging water. He loosed his grip and fell to the ground, coughing and spluttering.

He lay there on his back. Belle stood beside him watching her young master anxiously. Peter slowly closed his eyes. He could feel the warmth of the sun on his chilled skin. Suddenly he felt completely exhausted. He drifted off into sleep.

A bee buzzed close to Peter's ear. He opened his eyes. Above him the sky was blue as a butterfly's wing, a few soft clouds sailed across it like fleece. The golden sun embraced him with its warmth, there was a murmur of insects in the grass, he turned his head slightly and an angel came into view.

'I'm dead. This is paradise,' he thought and closed his eyes.

Then the angel kissed him. He felt her sweet breath on his lips. He opened his eyes again and looked into Elspeth's beautiful open laughing face, her green eyes radiant with happiness, her soft freckled skin haloed with her ridiculously unruly tangle of golden-red curls. He kissed her and he felt he had never done anything so tenderly in his whole life.

'She's the prettiest angel in heaven', he thought, 'and certainly the most fun. I wonder if I'm in love.'

'Now Elspeth, enough of this nuzzling, you have all your lives for it. One of us must go straight to William Salt to have his gashed leg treated. The other must presently take up her duties.'

Peter turned his head the other way and saw Henry standing on one leg, with his arm round Lucy's waist.

'Lucy, the Great Seal, where is it?' Peter remembered she had worn it on her ride through the city.

Lucy gave a light laugh, stretched her hand up and under Stang's saddle and pulled it out. 'I tucked it away there on my canter down to the harbour. Papa will be so pleased to see I still trust his old friend.'

Shortly the four of them, Lucy leading Belle with Henry in her saddle, Peter and Elspeth hand-in-hand

and leading Stang and Tench, left the beach and made their way slowly back to Nieuport. The beach where, three weeks later, a poor fisherman found, amongst the flotsam of the wreck, a fishing net. Caught up in the mesh was a beautiful Toledo blade with the inscribed initials PS and a magnificent pendant on a heavy gold chain. The medallion, that Ferdinand le Gray, that strong swimmer, had worn with such pride.

THE END

If you have enjoyed this story you will want to read the next one in the series, *A Pale Horse*. It is available as an e-book on i-books, Kindle, Kobo and The Nook.

From **A Pale Horse**
Chapter 1

A SUMMONS

'Her Royal Highness Princess Lucia and the Great Council of Voravia require her liege Peter Salt esquire to attend upon them at noon on Wednesday the seventeenth day of June for the purpose of the investiture of the said Peter Salt as a Knight of the Realm of Voravia.

Signed and dated this fifteenth day of June in the year of Our Lord 1535.'

There followed a very flowery signature that could just be discerned as *Lucia Regina.*

Along with the summons was a single sheet of parchment, folded, sealed and addressed to Peter Salt in the princess's own hand.

With great excitement Peter showed the formal command to his mother. The enclosure he stuffed into the belt of his breeches; he would open it in private.

'Oh Peter, your father will be so proud of you. I can't believe it! A knight of Voravia, here, in our little shop.' And Abigail threw her arms round her son.

It was not entirely a shock. As the originator of

the tactic that had led to an overwhelming victory he had rather expected some recognition but the delay had meant that he had begun to lose hope. Now, as is the way with a pleasure postponed, it was all the sweeter.

Abigail released her son as the door to the apothecary's shop opened.

'Ah here's your father, I can't wait to see his face!'

'Martley's due shortly, but I doubt there is much either Brother Simon or I can do for him now. The wound has healed, as has the bone, but I fear he will carry a limp for the rest of his life.'

'William, look at what's just arrived.' Abigail seized the summons from the counter and showed it to her husband. William read it.

'Congratulations, son. All Voravia knows you deserve this honour. Nevertheless, it is unexpected. Although, come to think of it, it is soldiers, whose business is killing, who get the knighthoods, not folk like Brother Simon whose business is saving lives and souls. They go unrewarded in this world. It was ever so.'

'But what is he to wear?' Abigail was already worrying that her son would not cut a fine enough figure when he appeared at court.

'I'll go in homespun linen. Lucy will expect it. I will never match the fine clothes of the courtiers however much we waste on silks and hose. No, I shall go as a soldier and I know of one man present who will think none the worse of me for doing so. Sir Walter

Martley is always very plainly dressed and everyone knows he is worth ten of your courtiers dressed in the height of fashion. I'll wear my Toledo blade, of course,' Peter added.

Also available on Kindle:

His Nation's Champion

Firepower

Winter